Doomsday Prepper Lessons

A Prepper's Guide to Surviving Catastrophe

By Ben Jakob

Doomsday Prepper Lessons

A Prepper's Guide to Surviving Catastrophe

By Ben Jakob

www.theprodoodler.com
Cover Design by The Pro Doodler

The Pro Doodler
Rockville, MD 20852
www.theprodoodler.com

Ordering Information:
Quantity sales: Special discounts are available on quantity purchases by corporations, associations, and others. For details, contact the publisher at the address above.
Printed in the United States of America

First Edition
14 13 12 11 10 / 10 9 8 7 6 5 4 3 2 1
ISBN #978-0-9905891-7-4

Doomsday
Prepper Lessons
A Prepper's Guide to
Surviving Catastrophe
Ben Jakob

ACKNOWLEDGEMENTS

No book of this magnitude would be complete without expressing thanks and appreciation to certain individuals.

First and foremost, I would like to humbly express my never-ending gratitude to the Big Boss, without whose help I would not be anything or have anything.

I would also like to thank my dear wife whose patience with me is unending. I thank her for allowing me the time and space to be able to write this book and bring it to the light of day.

Thank you to my honored parents and in-laws who have raised me and encouraged me and without whom I would not be the man I am.

Finally, I would like to say thank you to the following people:

L. Marcus for her encouragement and numerous suggestions.

I would also like to express appreciation to several friends who wish to remain anonymous.

DISCLAIMER

This book is for informational purposes only and is intended to provide information for a doomsday situation. It is sold with the understanding that neither the publisher nor the author is engaged in rendering legal, accounting, medical, mechanical, or other professional services. If legal or other expert assistance is required, the services of a competent professional should be sought.

The information contained in this publication are recommendations by the author, and reading this book does not guarantee your results will be the same as his.

The author disclaims all responsibility and liability for actions taken based on this communication.

The material herein includes information, products, and services by third parties. These do not necessarily mirror the opinions of the author.

The publication of such third-party materials does not constitute the author's guarantee of any information, opinion, products, or services from the third party material.

It is not the purpose of this book to be comprehensive and reprint all the information otherwise available to the public, but instead to complement, amplify, and supplement other texts. You are urged to read all available material, learn as much as possible, and tailor the information to your individual needs.

Every effort has been made to make this book as complete and as accurate as possible. However, there may be mistakes, both typographical and in content. Therefore, this text should be used only as a general guide and not as the ultimate source for prepper information. Furthermore, this book contains information on concrete bunker design and living that is current only up to the printing date. The purpose of this manual is to educate and entertain. The author and publisher shall have neither liability nor responsibility to any person or entity for any loss or damage caused, or alleged to have been caused, directly or indirectly, by the information contained in this book.

All medical and health-related information and materials contained herein are not intended to be a substitute for professional medical advice: it is being provided for general information purposes only. We make no representation and we assume no responsibility for the accuracy of any information contained in this book.

You will find many suggestions and thoughts about health issues. These statements have not been evaluated by the Food and Drug Administration. Nothing herein is intended to diagnose, treat, cure, or prevent any disease.

DEDICATION

This book is dedicated to:

All of the first responders, especially medical personnel who dedicate their lives to saving other people's lives at the risk of their safety.

OTHER TITLES BY BEN JAKOB

- Doomsday Bunker Book – On being prepared for a disaster
- Doomsday Bunker Book, Underground Edition – On being prepared for a disaster
- Addendums for Doomsday Bunker Book – On being prepared for a disaster
- CADD Manual for House Location Drawings – Written for a specific company, but adaptable for any company that uses CADD for house location drawings.
- Viduy – A translation of the Viduy written by the Chida, ZTL.
- The Quality of Light – A manual for photographers on lighting
- Kitchen Guide – Tips and tricks for the kitchen
- Not My People – A Historic Fiction Thriller novel 1976 – 1986

OTHER TITLES BY BEN JAKOB

- The Late Great Who? – The Sequel to Not My People 1987 – 1999
- Below the Surface – The conclusion

TABLE OF CONTENTS

TABLE OF CONTENTS

INTRODUCTION

As I type these words, we just got past the Coronavirus or Covid-19 pandemic, at least the first wave (assuming there will be a second wave).

Many panicked; stores ran out of basic supplies. Many died, many more were sick. Several of my friends had contracted the virus, and I lost a few people I knew. Before the pandemic, for twenty years, people made fun of me for being a prepper and a survivalist. During the first month or so after the outbreak, I was fielding calls daily from people apologizing to me for teasing me all those years. After that, many individuals contacted me asking for suggestions and aid to help them through the crisis. I did mention that during a crisis is not the time to start preparing, but there were some things that they could do to help them through the current predicament.

As I write, some people are speculating about a second wave. Some are saying that it will be worse than the first while others say that nothing will happen.

I do not preach one way or another, nor do I take any political position. I just like to look at what is going on, what has happened, and plan accordingly. By the time you read this, you will already know what happened regarding a second wave.

While Covid-19 was at its height, people asked me to give classes on how to be prepared for something like this in the future. I started doing research for those classes and taking copious notes for class lessons. This book is the culmination of that research that I can now distribute with the aim of helping a larger number of people.

OVER THE YEARS, PEOPLE HAVE asked me how and why I got into prepping. I would like to share with you the stories I have told others.

While I was growing up, my family was displaced by two hurricanes. We survived, but as a child, it was scary watching the floodwaters encroach upon and take over our house and the neighborhood. We stayed with friends for a few weeks and the cleanup was grueling.

Because of where we lived, my parents had a cold storage room in the basement where they kept many cans of assorted foods. I remember my grandmother canning some of it.

If you have read my previous book, Doomsday Bunker Book, I describe how to design and ultimately live in either an underground or an aboveground bunker. That book came about because of a client who wanted me to design a similar bunker for him. I was already a prepper by that time, but that is when I started to take things more seriously.

There have been many times in my life that I have been without. Many times the electricity has gone out, sometimes for days or even weeks.

INTRODUCTION

At one time in my life, I lived at the top of a mountain far from civilization. I have been snowbound on top of that mountain with no access to public services or outside interventions for weeks on end.

Besides, let us not forget the recent pandemic.

I am not an expert, but I have some knowledge that I would like to share with you.

Most of the information herein can and has been culled from the Internet. I have put into practice and done everything I discuss. I did all of this research for you and put it all together in one place for you to make your life easier. I hope that you can use this book as a reference and guide for many years to come.

I have a friend who is a prepper and lost his job several years ago. He asked me, "Since I have no income, would it be prudent for me to use my prepper supplies and food?"

I told him, "That was the reason to be a prepper, to have for instances when one does not have." To me, it is no different from having a "rainy day fund".

Like all preppers, I hope that we never need to go to the extremes mentioned below, but it is always a good idea to be prepared, especially if you have a family to protect and provide for.

In this book, there are many suggestions and thoughts about health issues. These statements have not been evaluated by the Food and Drug Administration. Nothing herein is intended to diagnose, treat, cure, or prevent any disease.

TIPS

Before we get started, I would like to share with you some tips to help make your life easier and more comfortable.

Always remember, "One is none and two is one". Meaning, always have a backup and even several backups. This is essential because inevitably something will break, get lost, or wear out.

You should start collecting fire starters and combustibles: dryer lint, crayons, pine needles, toilet paper tubes, paper towel tubes, commercial fire starters, flint, and I even heard that matches can be used to start fires.

When things started getting serious with Covid-19, people ran to the store to buy toilet paper. People were hoarding so much that for weeks there was none on the shelves. After a few weeks, I saw only cheap one-ply TP, that I would not use, that was selling for almost double what it used to cost. While people were desperate for TP, I counted my inventory and found that I had about 200 rolls stocked up in my main location, not including my bugout locations. I was not worried.

Here are some basic tips to help get you started.

- Do not ignore your physical or spiritual health.
- Get a Ham radio (Amateur Radio) license and a 2-meter radio. This is much better than a CB radio. You can have a Ham radio without a license; you just cannot transmit (talk).
- A pet will give you some comfort, entertainment, company, help your mood, health, and much more. A large dog will also help you with security. (There is nothing so warm as a cold wet nose.)
- Used tea bags can be used as air fresheners.
- Get a drone to be aware of what is going on around you
- Have a supply of non-battery-operated games, books, and toys
- Learn first aid and CPR
- Become CERT (Community Emergency Response Team) certified.
- Try to put together a clique of similarly minded folks who can get together and help one another prepping and surviving in a crisis
- Practice bugging out
- Practice bugging in
- While things are quiet, learn as much as you can about prepping. Practice everything in this book that you can until it is second nature.
- Learn how to make hand sanitizer. (2/3 alcohol and 1/3 aloe vera gel)
- See your doctors and dentist, have two pairs of glasses, and enough medicines to last a year.
- Set up an aquaponics garden (see <u>Doomsday Bunker Book</u>)

- Learn gardening
- When you go shopping, but one extra item that you need and put it in your prepper pantry. When you buy TP, buy a few extra rolls and store them.
- Rotate your stock; do not let anything get stale.
- Buy what you use and eat and use and eat what you buy
- Learn how to conserve and reuse as much as possible. I will give you an example below.
- Learn how to tie different types of knots. Different types of knots are used for different purposes, but this is not the medium to teach you knots. Just to list a few:
    - Figure 8 knot
    - Clove hitch
    - Bowline
    - Half hitch
    - Double half hitch
    - Half knot
    - Noose
    - Overhand knot
    - Sheet bend
    - Taut line hitch
    - Slip knot
    - Square knot

CONSERVE

I mentioned above that you should learn how to conserve and reuse as much as possible. For example, when you cut peppers, what do you do with the seeds and top of the pepper? If you are typical, you will do what most people do and throw it in the trash.

From now on, you will put it into a Ziploc bag and put it in the freezer.

The part of the stem of broccoli and cauliflower put in the same bag. What about the peal from an onion? Do the same, put it in a Ziploc bag in the freezer.

All parts of fruits and vegetables that you would normally discard, put into the same bag in the freezer. Even produce that is about to spoil, put it in the same bag.

When you have a sufficient amount, wrap the contents into a cheesecloth and put it into a large pot. Fill the pot with water and bring it to a boil. Let it simmer all day. Remove the cheesecloth and the vegetables and set aside.

The broth is what I use as a base for soups and stews, instead of the powders that are filled with sodium and chemicals. I then take the broth and can it and put it in my pantry.

The reserve vegetables I put through a food processor and remove any pieces that did not grind up completely. Sometimes that is part of the peel from the onion or a seed from an orange.

Then I add some breadcrumbs, eggs, and seasonings and make vegetable patties in my air fryer. If you do not have an air fryer, a frying pan will work fine. You get the idea.

My point is that nothing was wasted and I have healthier alternatives to feed my family.

Time

You can use a wristwatch to determine the points of a compass. It is important to note that the method changes depending on if you are in the northern or southern hemisphere, if it is before or after 12 pm and if it is Daylight Savings Time.

Northern Hemisphere

With the watch level to the ground, point the hour hand toward the sun. The midway point between the hour hand and 12 pm is due south. In other words, if the hour hand is at 2, then south is at 1 o'clock.

Southern Hemisphere

Again with the watch level to the ground, this time point the 12 toward the sun. The bisection of 12 and the hour hand will be due south.

Time of Day

If you are measuring before 12 pm, the bisection between the hour hand and 12 should be made clockwise. Conversely, if it is after 12 pm, measure counterclockwise.

FINALLY, REMEMBER TO ADJUST AN hour if it is currently Daylight Savings Time on your watch.

SAYINGS

The following are some common sayings about prepping. There are thousands, but these are the ones that I like the best. I have tried to find out who originally said these things but for the most part, was unable to.

- Buy what you eat and eat what you buy.
- By failing to prepare, you are preparing to fail.
    - Benjamin Franklin
- Two is one and one is none
- Be prepared, not scared
- Remember, when Noah built the ark, it was not yet raining
- I am my own FEMA, I am a prepper
- First In, First Out
- The first rule of prepper club, “Never talk about prepper club.”
- Hope for the best, prepare for the worst.

TERMS

This chapter is to share with you some of the common terms that are bandied about by people in the prepping/survivalist community. This list is far from comprehensive but contains those terms that I believe are most important.

ALICE

ALICE is an acronym for **All-Purpose Lightweight Individual Carrying Equipment** and is a pack system invented by the military for the efficient carrying of supplies. The transporting material is not only convenient but allows you to carry everything you could need. This system was replaced by the MOLLE; see further in this list.

BIVY

Bivy sack is short for **bivouac sack**. It was invented to serve climbers who wanted lightweight, emergency weather protection for sleeping bags during multi-day ascents.

BOB

BOB is an acronym for **Bug Out Bag**. Bug out bag refers to a bag that could be a backpack or a duffle bag or any other style of portable container. What is important in this context is its content. It consists mainly of emergency materials that you need to survive during or after a disaster.

If it is prepared with a time frame of three days, it is often referred to as a 72-hour kit; however, BOB normally contains supplies that can keep you going indefinitely. These include a first aid kit, weapons/ammo, cash, water, water filter, sleeping bag, emergency medicine, clothing, means of identification, etc. Also, BOB tends to be a relative concept and is customized to include different things for individual needs.

BOL

BOL is an acronym that stands for **Bug Out Location**. This is a place other than a home in which the survivalist can retreat in times of danger or crisis. These retreats should be independently sufficient so that you are not stranded while you secure yourself from danger. Normally, it is located in scarcely populated rural areas as a BOL involves having a safe place to retreat from the dangers that are more likely to plague urban areas.

I recommend having one hidden, fully stocked BOL. You should practice packing up and bugging out to your BOL.

I also recommend having a secondary location you can go to for shelter. In this case, maybe have a few emergency buckets buried. Even if this is public land, in an emergency scenario, you can hide there for a time.

BUGGING IN

Bugging in means to stay at a specific current location until it is safe to move out. Although, it depends on the kind of SHTF situation, when in crisis, bugging in, alongside bugging out, is among the first actions preppers consider.

Bugging in usually refers to staying put in one's home or apartment and securing the location as best as possible.

BUGGING OUT

This means moving away from a current position and moving to a safer location. It is a military term that directly means to retreat, or more specifically, to flee in panic.

CME

C.M.E stands for **Coronal Mass Ejection**. A coronal mass ejection is a significant release of plasma and the accompanying magnetic field from the solar (sun's) corona. They often follow solar flares and normally occur during a solar prominence eruption. The plasma is released through the solar wind and can cause electrical and meteorological disturbances on Earth.

EDC

This is usually translated as **Everyday Carry**. It refers to the things a person carries on them daily. Depending on the individual, it might include anything from a firearm to items as basic as a cell phone, or even a handkerchief.

EMP

E.M.P stands for **Electromagnetic Pulse** can be a natural or artificial occurrence. It usually occurs in a radiated, electric or magnetic field and is usually hazardous to electronic equipment and other infrastructure depending upon the magnitude of the energy.

FARADAY CAGE

This refers to a metal casing that protects a person's electronics from an EMP. It is formed from conductive materials and insulation and is used to block electric fields.

FIFO

This is an acronym that stands for **First In, First Out**. It is a method used in food storage and food rotation. It involves using items that are first stored before consuming the more recently stored ones. It does not refer only to food; it could also be for medicines or other types of items that have a limited shelf life.

FUBAR

F*ed Up Beyond All Recognition**

GHB

Get Home Bag for when there is a situation that requires you to get home in an atypical manner. This typically means getting home by foot so what you have in your GHB should last you for a few days, or however long you think it will take you to get home.

GOLDEN HORDE

This term is synonymous with Zombies and is used to describe a group of fleeing people who are so unprepared and desperate that they loot everything in their path in a WROL situation.

GOOD

Get Out Of Dodge is a term that refers to the process of getting out of a bad or/and dangerous situation.

HAM

A term used to refer to amateur radio or its operators. It is used to refer to people who use equipment to create two-way communication with other people on radio frequencies that are assigned to the amateur radio service by the Federal Communications Commission.

IFAK

Stands for **Individual First-Aid Kit**. Typically, this includes medical supplies that help the avoidance of preventable deaths or to treat deep injuries.

INCH

This is an acronym that represents a short message code for your family and/or friends in case you have to bug out. It means, **I'm Not Coming Home**.

MOLLE

MOLLE stands for **Modular Lightweight Load-Carrying Equipment:** a convenient system invented by the military for bugging out. It replaced the ALICE system.

MRE

This is an acronym that stands for **Meal Ready-to-Eat**. It is a self-contained ration with lightweight packaging that is meant for an individual. Typically, they can last for years and are great for when other food is unavailable. Depending upon the meal, the MRE might come with a mini-heating element. They also contain cutlery and napkins.

OPSEC

It is an abbreviation for **Operational Security**. Its general idea is to keep your activities and any other vital information as secret as possible with a view to deprive the enemy of any helpful data.

POLLYANNA

This is someone who is naïvely optimistic, even when there is trouble or when SHTF.

PERK

This is an acronym for **Personal Emergency Relocation Kit**. This is a variant of a BOB that is used for an emergency relocation, maybe in a retreat from imminent danger.

Although preppers usually carry EDC's which include things needed in day to day activities, Bug Out Bags (See BOB above), and Personal Survival Kit (See PSK below), PERK is a set of items that are specifically needed for an emergency retreat.

PREP

Prep is a shortened version of the word "prepare".

PREPPER

This term describes an individual who is always prepared for an emergency.

PSK

This is an acronym that means **Personal Survival Kit**. It involves items needed to survive in harsh conditions. The kit contains signaling items, including rescue reflectors, emergency whistles, rescue laser, flare, and emergency devices which can include a pocket chainsaw, survival candle, fishing kit, and sewing kit.

SHEEPLE

Sheeple refers to people who always follow the crowd and are mostly unable to think for themselves.

SHTF

S* Hits The Fan** is a term that preppers use to describe catastrophic events. Examples of such events are natural and man-made disasters like earthquakes, pandemics, terrorist attacks, and financial collapse.

SURVIVALIST

A survivalist is someone who has knowledge and skill to survive on his/her own for a time. For example, hunting, fishing, fire starting, first aid, finding water, and more.

TEOTWAWKI

TEOTWAWKI is a term mostly used online by survivalists. It means "**The End Of The World As We Know It**". TEOTWAWKI is often synonymous with SHTF.

WROL

The term is an acronym for "**Without Rule of law**". WROL is a term that is used to describe a situation in which the police and every institutional body that functions to uphold the law have lost control. The police and other LEO's[1] have lost all control resulting in a lawless environment. These situations mostly occur after intense catastrophic happenings or during riots.

YOYO

You are On Your Own

ZOMBIE

See Golden Horde above

[1] Law Enforcement Officer

TYPES OF SITUATIONS

There are many types of situations and scenarios people prepare for, some are realistic, some less so. Here are just a few of the more common scenarios that we might encounter. Sometimes the situation is more serious than expected, sometimes less so. That is why we are preppers: to prepare for what may come.

A friend of mine whom I taught to be a prepper had a decent stock of supplies and was able to stay in his house for several months when Covid-19 hit. He was prepared with everything he needed.

In many of the scenarios that follow, an underground or at least an aboveground bunker would be the best option to protect yourself and your loved ones.

Cyberattack

A cyberattack is any attempt to expose, alter, disable, destroy, steal, or gain unauthorized access to or make unauthorized use of a computer or computer network asset.

Cyberattacks are normally conducted by hacking.

Cessation of Public Services

Many of the doomsday scenarios listed here may lead to public services being unavailable or discontinued in some fashion.

EMP

Electromagnetic Pulse is a short burst of electromagnetic energy. Such a pulse's origin may be a natural occurrence or man-made and can occur as a radiated, electric, or magnetic field or a conducted electric current, depending on the source.

An EMP will in all probability take out all electrical appliances and equipment.

Flooding

A hurricane, a collapsed dam, or other major natural event can cause flooding. During such an occurrence, water will not be drinkable, electricity will probably not work and other public services (e.g., emergency services) will be unavailable.

Financial Collapse

Many disasters could lead to a financial collapse, which could lead to marauding and rioting. The stock market could plunge, prices rise, stores gouging prices on products, and other ways of financial distress.

Nuclear

Read my book, Doomsday Bunker Book on what to do in the event of a nuclear attack. Depending on the distance from the epicenter, the altitude, and magnitude of the explosion, one could survive if one knows what to do and how to decontaminate oneself.

Pandemic

Covid-19. Need I say more?

Rioting

I do not care what side of the political spectrum you are on, protesting and rioting are two disparate things. If there are violence and destruction, then it is rioting and the rioters should be arrested. Breaking into stores and destroying property is rioting and we need to be prepared to protect ourselves and our property.

Shortages

After any major catastrophic event, there are going to be shortages of supplies, food, and medicine. The prices will likely double or worse for what is left on store shelves.

Societal Collapse

Rioting mentioned above, and marauding are just two examples of societal collapse.

Solar Flare

It is caused by a coronal mass ejection from the sun and can wreak havoc on planet Earth. Significant weather changes, disruption of power, utilities and more can lead to TEOTWAWKI.

War

A war would devastate any country and economy. It does not matter if it is a local skirmish or an all-out war between two factions or countries. I do not have to tell you the destruction, annihilation, and carnage that would ensue. Having a remote bugout location would be useful in the event of a war.

Weather

Anything from snow to tornadoes, flooding to earthquakes, could send people and the economy into panic mode. Having a remote bugout location would be a life-saver for you and your loved ones.

THINGS TO PURCHASE

You probably came across this book because you are a prepper or a survivalist or experienced an event (like Covid-19) where you were forced to re-evaluate your priorities.

If you are new to the prepping community, you will find this list invaluable. If you have been in the community for some time, you are probably familiar with the basics, for example, water, water purification, food, first aid, matches, and flashlights. However, even experienced preppers may overlook some things, so I put together this list to help you. This does not encompass everything possible; however, it is a good start and should tickle your brain to think of other things. This is not a bugout list, which you will find toward the end of this book. Rather, this is a tally of supplies to help you start stocking up to prepare for a doomsday scenario. Most of these items will be mentioned further in this book.

THINGS TO PURCHASE

- **5 GALLON BUCKETS** – For storage, water, and much more. When storing food, use only food-grade buckets.
- **ALCOHOL** – For cleaning and antiseptic purposes.
- **ALUMINUM FOIL** – There are so many uses for aluminum foil, including cooking, covering, packing, signaling, and much more.
- **Ammunition** – Make sure you have a good stock of ammunition because, without it, your guns are just paperweights.
- **APPLE CIDER VINEGAR** – Good for food and has many health benefits.
- **AX** – For chopping wood.
- **BABY WIPES** – A great way to keep clean without using any precious water.
- **BATTERIES** – A large assortment and supply of each size and voltage.
- **BICYCLE** – If you need transportation but do not want to, or cannot, use gasoline.
- **BICYCLE GEAR** – You will need supplies and tools to maintain your bike.
- **BIVY** – A type of lightweight sleeping bag and tent.
- **BLINDFOLD** – If you are a light sleeper, the sun may bother you in the early morning, and if you are taking a nap during the afternoon.
- **BOOKS** – As many paper books and reading material as you can get your hands on.
- **BOOTS** – For rain and snow.
- **BOW AND ARROW** – For hunting and protection.
- **CALENDAR** – Paper calendar. You will want something with several years in the future to be able to keep track of time.
- **CAN OPENER** – Mechanical can opener.
- **CANDLES** – For light and heat.

- **CANDY** – Have some around to help break the monotony, but not too much.
- **CAST IRON POTS AND PANS** – If you are cooking over a fire, regular pots and pans will not work.
- **CELL PHONE BATTERIES** – Have a few external phone batteries to extend the life of your cell phone and tablet.
- **CHARCOAL BRIQUETTES** – To help make a fire for cooking.
- **CINNAMON** – Cinnamon has many health benefits.
- **CLOCK** – Get a mechanical version that does not require batteries.
- **CLOTH DIAPERS** – They are great for many things as they are very absorbent.
- **CLOTHESPINS** – You may not be able to use a clothes dryer. Besides, they have many other uses.
- **COFFEE** – Most people drink coffee and it may also be used for barter.
- **COMPASS** – For use with a map to be able to navigate without GPS.
- **CONDIMENTS** – They are going to help enhance your meals, and they are also great for barter.
- **CONDOMS** – Aside from the obvious, they are great for storing and protecting things and are very expandable.
- **COTTON BALLS** – First aid, hygiene, cleanup, kindling, and much more.
- **DISPOSABLE CUTLERY** – After you use them, they can be thrown away without wasting water by washing them.
- **DISPOSABLE DISHES** – After you use them, they can be burned and not waste precious water.

THINGS TO PURCHASE

- **DUCT TAPE** – You can never have enough duct tape. I dedicate a complete chapter herein to duct tape.
- **EARPLUGS** – If you are sleeping in the woods, nature's noises may disturb your sleep. If you use them while sleeping, make sure someone is awake for protection.
- **EYEWEAR** – Glasses, contacts, backup, repair kits, supplies.
- **FEMININE HYGIENE** – Have a good supply on hand.
- **FIRST AID SUPPLIES** – Get as much as you can.
- **FISHING KIT** – You will probably want to eat and fish are plentiful and healthy.
- **FLARE GUN** – For your protection and emergency signaling.
- **FLOSS** – Make sure to take care of your dental needs. Floss is also a very good and durable replacement for a string.
- **FLOWERPOT HEATER** – Learn how to make one from my book, Doomsday Bunker Book.
- **GAMES** – You will want to have as many games as possible that do not require electricity or batteries. Do NOT neglect this.
- **GAS MASK** – In case the air becomes contaminated or difficult to breathe.
- **GASOLINE** – To fill your vehicle and generator.
- **GENERATOR** – There are many options, consider wisely. Gas-powered, propane-powered, solar-powered, and dual fuel options
- **GLOW STICKS** – They are great for giving you light at night and helping you navigate in the dark. It is safer for a child to use a glow stick than a candle.
- **GOGGLES** – Safety first
- **HAND WARMERS** – You may not have access to heat.

- **HAND SANITIZER** – Great for cleaning anything, especially if you do not have free water. Learn how to make it.
- **HAND SOAP** – I prefer liquid soap as opposed to bar soap but that is a personal preference.
- **HONEY** – Honey is the one natural food that does not spoil and it has many health benefits.
- **INSECT REPELLENT** – You are going to want to keep the bugs at bay.
- **KITCHEN SUPPLIES** – Spatulas, tongs, ladles, pots, pans, plates, bowls, etc.
- **KITTY LITER** – To absorb spills and smells and for traction in the snow.
- **KNIVES** – For hunting, protection, and much more. Have several different types and sizes.
- **LANTERNS** – Get both propane and battery-operated versions.
- **LIGHTER FLUID** – To help with starting fires for cooking and heat.
- **MAP** – Get several maps of your immediate area, town, state, and county. GPS may not always be working, but paper maps will.
- **MEDICINE** – You will want a stock of your medicine and vitamins. Do not forget your pets.
- **MOUTH WASH** – You will want to feel fresh.
- **MRE** – Meals Ready to Eat. There are many brands and kits. Check them out and taste them to find the types you enjoy.
- **MUSICAL INSTRUMENT** – Used for entertainment and to help keep up morale. Get instruments that do not require batteries or electricity.
- **NYLON ROPE** – You will use this for hanging laundry, tying things down, and much more.
- **PAPER TOWELS** – To help clean up messes.
- **PARACORD** – Is used instead of regular rope but it is much better. Paracord can be

disassembled and the strands can be used for many things.

- **PENCIL/PEN AND PAPER** – Remember, computers may not be working and you will probably want to keep a journal, write notes or letters.
- **PEPPER SPRAY** – For protection
- **PET SUPPLIES** – Do not forget your furry friends. Do NOT abandon them. Make sure you have enough food, medicine, and supplies for them.
- **PLAYING CARDS** – For entertainment.
- **PLANT SEEDS** – To be able to grow plants.
- **PLASTIC WRAP** – Aside from food needs, the plastic wrap may be used for many other purposes. Get several large sizes. Larger sizes can be used for repairs, collecting water, as an air barrier, and more.
- **POTASSIUM IODIDE** – To protect your thyroid in case of nuclear contamination.
- **POTTED PLANTS** – You will want to eat and it is easier to grow tomatoes, lettuce, and more in a pot than in the ground.
- **POWDERED EGGS** – Eggs are great, but they do not store for a very long time. However, powdered eggs can last indefinitely.
- **POWDERED DRINKS** – They are easier to carry, and take up less space, than a bottle of liquid drink.
- **POWDERED MILK** – Milk is great but does not store for very long.
- **PROPANE** – For your propane devices.
- **PROPANE GRILL** – For cooking.
- **PROPANE HEATER** – For heating.
- **PROPANE STOVE** – For cooking.
- **PUP TENT** – For emergency outdoor sleeping.
- **RAIN GEAR** – For rain protection.
- **REFLECTIVE VEST** – Safety first

- **RUBBER GLOVES** – For protection and cleanliness.
- **SALT** – There are many uses for salt, aside from cooking. I dedicate a complete chapter to salt.
- **SAW** – Once you chop the wood, you will need a saw.
- **SEASONINGS** – You do not want to eat bland food, and seasonings can be used for barter.
- **SEWING KIT** – Clothes will tear and other things will need repair.
- **SHOELACES** – Aside from the obvious, they have several other uses.
- **SHOVEL** – Get both a digging shovel and a snow shovel.
- **SLEEPING BAG** – For emergency sleeping outside and is a good overall blanket.
- **SOUP POWDERS** – For spicing up your foods and great for barter.
- **SPORTS** – Have something available to help divert your attention. Consider a football, basketball, and baseball equipment.
- **STERNO FUEL** – For cooking and heating purposes.
- **STUN GUN** – For protection.
- **SURVIVAL BOOKS** – There are many available and you should have a few for reference, like this one.
- **TACTICAL PEN** – Great pen, tool, and weapon.
- **TARP** – Can be used for water collection, protection, ground cover, shade, and much more.
- **THERMAL BLANKET** – A light-weight blanket that will help keep you warm.
- **TOILET PAPER** – As much as you can horde, and then get some more.
- **TOOLS** – Get as many types of hand tools as possible.

THINGS TO PURCHASE

- **TRASH BAGS** – Storage, water, trash, raincoat, and more.
- **VINEGAR** – There are many uses for vinegar.
- **WALKIE TALKIE** – For communication.
- **WATER PURIFICATION TABLETS** – You will never know the condition of the water.
- **WATER STRAW** – You will never know the condition of the water.
- **WEAPONS** – There are many types of weapons one can purchase. Make sure you have a variety, and more importantly, know how to use them.
- **WHISTLES** – For protection and communication.
- **ZIPLOC BAGS** – Protect and organize your food and supplies.
- **ZEER FRIDGE** – Learn how to make one from my book, Doomsday Bunker Book.

WATER

Finding, storing, and filtering water go hand in hand. Preppers live by this dictum: a person can live about three weeks without food, but only about three days without water.

Most people fail to stock enough water, though some may have stocked adequate water filtration methods. You should have both, a good supply of water and several methods of cleaning your water. It is necessary to have a supply of water not only for drinking but also for cooking and cleaning. Additionally, preppers need to know how to source water and filter it.

A water strategy includes obtaining, storing, filtering, purifying, and sanitizing water. You need to start early with your water preps and stock as much as possible. What follows is your water survival guide.

WATER

Bottled Water

Bottled water is your first defense. Think about this: the cheapest, fastest, and the best thing you can do for your survival is to have bottled water on hand. If you do not have several jugs of water, then get some immediately.

Obtaining bottled water is only your first step: for the long term, you will need to source more water and learn to filter it. You will also need practical water storage options for larger quantities. That said, obtaining bottled water is the fastest and easiest way to start prepping.

Bottled water can last indefinitely, however, it is a good idea to rotate your bottled water stock to maintain a better-tasting supply of water.

That does not mean all bottled water has no chemicals. Read labels and look for water without fluoride and other additives such as minerals added for flavoring.

Storing your water can present challenges. Below are some tips to help you with your water storage.

- Store bottled water in a cool dry place, away from sunlight, and not resting directly on cement, which could leach chemicals into your water.
- Avoid stacking jugs, cases, or boxes of water too high. Large cases may put too much pressure on the bottom cases which will eventually give way and leak. You do not want water damage to your home.
    - Water weighs about 8.3 pounds per gallon.
- Rotate your stock and check it often to ensure your water reserves are adequate.

- Drink bottled water within three days of opening to minimize the risk of contamination with microbiological pathogens or molds.
- Purchase fifty-five-gallon water barrels.
- Purchase IBC's for water storage (I discuss this in more detail later).

NOTE: Do NOT reuse disposable water, juice, milk, or soda bottles. Most of these are made of polyethylene terephthalate, also known as PETE. While these bottles are safe for one-time use, they may leach DEHP (a carcinogen) when used repeatedly.

Stock, Stock, and Stock

I hope that you will never need to use a water siphon, or a fire hydrant wrench to get your water because you will need much more water than you think. However, you should have those tools just in case.

In addition to drinking water, you will also need to store water for reconstituting dried foods (cooking pasta, freeze-dried meals, rice, and beans), cleaning dishes and utensils, and for bathing. (Remember also to store for pets and livestock). Having a personal water filter for everyone is important not only for the bugout bag, but for your "get home bag," at the office or school, and in your vehicle(s).

The effects of dehydration run the gamut of lethargy, loss of mental alertness, headaches, urinary tract infections, and kidney stones. Even if you are an advanced prepper and think you know everything about water and hydration, consider this important fact: you will need at least one gallon per person per day.

How much water should a person store? Ninety gallons is a three-month supply of water for one person. If there are others in the party, it does not necessarily mean you multiply the number, but it is a good idea to do so. Group activities, such as washing dishes, will consolidate the numbers a bit, but generally, you should count on ninety gallons per person for three months.

Your bathtub is a good last-minute place to store water. Filling the bathtub (assuming it is clean) is one of the first things to do immediately following an electromagnetic pulse or some similar catastrophic event.

A standard residential water heater is only forty or fifty gallons, which is not nearly enough. I recommend storing five fifty-five-gallon barrels. Make sure they are food grade barrels. Storage of the same amount of water in less space than five barrels would be to utilize an Intermediate Bulk Container (IBC).

You will need purification systems for your BOB, Get Home Bag, car, BOL, and more.

Water Purification

Either you prepare water, or you prepare for medical complications. Preppers make it a priority to learn about water purification and filtration methods for their survival. There are several methods to make water safe for drinking.

Realistically, you will need several water purification systems. It is important to know which contaminants are present in your specific area so you can be prepared to appropriately decontaminate your water.

- **Boiling water**. The oldest method of water purification is boiling water for ten minutes. Boiling does not guarantee good tasting water; this is why, back in the day, people drank tea and beer.
- **Gravel, sand, and charcoal**. Layer a sock or straining container with charcoal at the

bottom, then sand and gravel at the top, and filter your water into a container. This method will make the water taste better and filter out some bacteria and small particles.

- **Chlorination**. According to FEMA, chlorinating water will kill most micro-organisms. There are three methods to purify water through chlorination.
    - **Chlorine dioxide** tablets and drops.
    - **Chlorine bleach**. Ten drops of bleach per gallon are all that is needed. Shake the container and wait thirty minutes. Check the chapter on Bleach for more information.
    - **Filtration**. Filtering water provides the essential benefits of removing disease-causing parasites. You can also filter fluoride, arsenic, and other contaminants out of the water by using a water filter.

Hidden Water

When the faucets stop bringing water, pay attention to these hidden water sources:

- Rainwater[2]
- Rivers
- Streams
- Ponds
- Lakes
- Springs
- Hot water tank
- Toilet storage, or reserve tank
- Ice cube trays

---

[2] Collecting rainwater is prohibited in many states.

- Fire Hydrant

Tap Water Has Chemicals and Contaminants.

Be water safe and water smart. Your tap water may contain lead, arsenic, fluoride, nitrates, sulfates, radon, and other chemicals and contaminants.

Get the facts about your local tap water and start filtering it. Every locale has its contaminants and problems; you should learn what is in yours.

- Learn the difference between hard and soft water.
  - **Hard Water**. Hard water has high mineral content. Hard water is formed when water percolates through deposits of limestone, chalk or gypsum, which are largely made up of calcium and magnesium carbonates, bicarbonates.
  - **Soft Water**. Surface water contains low concentrations of ions, in particular, calcium and magnesium. Soft water naturally occurs where rainfall and the drainage basin of rivers are formed of hard, impervious, and calcium-poor rocks.
- Find out about other contaminants lurking in your tap water (specific to your town or region).

Water to Avoid

Not all water is fit for drinking, so be careful what you drink.

- Do not drink water from the toilet reserve tank. This is not suitable for drinking water because of cleaning agent contaminants that may have been used. Previous tenants may have used toilet tank cleaning agents, rendering this water undrinkable.

- Do not drink water from the car or home radiators because of contaminants.
- Do not drink water from waterbeds because of the chemicals.
- Do not drink water from chemically treated pools and spas
- Do not drink floodwaters, as these are contaminated with chemicals and bacteria from spills.
- Do not use well water until you have it tested.
- Do not drink un-distilled saltwater.

Prepare Water Today

Prepare for your family today, by harnessing and collecting freshwater for tomorrow. The time to build a well is not when you are thirsty. Below you will find a few additional ideas on water storage:

- Learn how to use gray water and rainwater systems, rain barrels, tanks, and other water storage techniques for household and emergency use.
- There are many sizes and shapes of storage tanks on the market. Do your research for what works best for you and your situation.
- Water can be stored in tanks, bricks, jugs, and barrels
- IBC's (Intermediary Bulk Container) come in two different sizes: 275 and 330 gallons.
- Personal water towers (smaller versions of what cities use to store water for emergencies.)

Conserve Water

- Do not eat salty foods in time of extreme water shortage, as these will make you thirstier; however, recognize that you need sodium and that it is lost in sweat and urine.
- Consult your physician and consider an electrolyte supplement. These are used in endurance training and can assist in your survival.
- Do not brush your teeth with the last of the water.
- Do not shave with a razor and water, as you want to conserve water.
- Stock up and use lip balms to soothe dry lips and lotions for providing additional moisture.
- Store disposable cups for hot and cold drinks, plus disposable plastic utensils and paper plates to avoid using drinking water to wash dishes.

Fire

I know, you are wondering why I would put a section on fire in the chapter of water. They do not appear to go together.

However, if you have a fire, even controlled, you should have the means to extinguish it. The obvious way is with water, but when you have a catastrophic situation, water is a precious commodity.

I mention elsewhere in this book that you should have a fire extinguisher on hand. However, remember, if there is an emergency, your water may also be needed to extinguish a fire and that will significantly reduce your water reserves.

I will share with you something that I helped a colleague build. He and I lived in an area where the fire department was nicknamed "chimney savers." It was not to be disparaging of the fire department, but rather they were so far away that by the time they arrived at a conflagration, the only thing remaining to save would be the brick chimney.

Together we assembled an aboveground twenty-four-foot round pool that was about four feet deep. It held about twelve-thousand gallons of water that was filled mostly by rainwater (some direct and some diverted).

The pool was located at a higher elevation than the house. Gravity-fed pipes along with a few pumps and hoses were all it took to make the system work. With the addition of a few backup batteries to power the pumps, everything was set.

Final Thoughts

Water is the most crucial element of survival. Learn about the potential risks of bottled and tap water and what you can do to stay happy, healthy, and hydrated.

No electricity = no water

Remember, it takes electricity to pipe water to the faucets in your home. A big threat to the water supply is an electricity shortage caused by an Electromagnetic Pulse (EMP), which could cause water scarcity for months on end. Do not count on the government to supply you with water, because an EMP will immobilize all vehicles. This means batteries for virtually all cars, trucks, and ATVs will be useless.

Even if electricity and water are flowing in your municipality, contamination of your water may occur at the source after natural disasters (earthquakes, hurricanes, or tornadoes) or man-made ones.

WATER

In short, preppers must

- Store as much water as possible
- Constantly monitor the supplies for leakage
- Stock more water than for anticipated needs
- Purchase and learn how to use water testing kits
- Filter water and test for impurities
- Source additional water supplies (water heater, fire hydrant, lakes, etc.)
- Know what water to avoid, including certain bottled waters
- Plan today for tomorrow's water needs

FOODS TO STOCK

This chapter will help you decide what foods you should stock in advance of an emergency or catastrophe. This is my list; yours will differ based on your geographic location and familial needs. Keep in mind the individual tastes of your family and clique.

It is not easy to start prepping. With the help of this book, I hope to make it a bit easier for you. The easiest way to start prepping is to purchase an extra item or two whenever you go shopping for your regular needs. For example, when you buy tuna fish cans, buy a couple of extra cans and put them in your prepper pantry. When you buy mayonnaise, buy an extra jar and put it in the pantry. Next time you need toothpaste, buy an extra tube. You get the idea.

Keep in mind, only purchase what you use and use what you purchase. Always rotate your stock so that nothing gets old or stale. Equally important is checking the ingredients of all the food you store and eat. You do not want empty calories and sugars.

Storage

I am often asked where to store all the items we prep. I live in a small apartment so I have had to innovate. Here are a few ideas for you.

- Top of a closet
- A shelf in the laundry room
- Build shelves around the perimeter of rooms
- Under beds
- Elevate your bed a few inches to get more storage room under the bed
- Do you have a spare shower or bathtub? Build shelves
- Rent a storage unit
- An outdoor shed

Beans and Legumes

Stock up on beans - all kinds of dried beans and canned beans. The more variety of beans you store, the better, as they provide energy and fiber. Beans pack around 1250 calories per pound. Best of all, you can sprout beans – in as few as five days you will have crunchy, fresh phytonutrients for your family from dried beans, peas, and lentils.

Bragg's Apple Cider Vinegar

Stock a couple of bottles of vinegar, specifically apple cider vinegar. Bragg's organic apple cider vinegar is so useful you will want one for your pantry and one for your medicine cabinet.

- All you need is apple cider vinegar, oil, salt, and pepper to make a simple salad dressing and marinade.
- You can add apple cider vinegar to your morning smoothie for a healthful boost.
- While apple cider vinegar is the king of vinegar, stock balsamic vinegar, cider vinegar, and rice wine as well.
- Apple cider vinegar has a multitude of healthful benefits; there are plenty of other reasons to stock it with your prepping supplies.

Breadcrumbs and Stuffing

Breadcrumbs are a satisfying addition to casseroles and a nice addition to salmon and crab cakes you can make with the cans in your food storage. Unfortunately, it is difficult to find breadcrumbs sealed in plastic for freshness. Ideally, you should make your breadcrumbs and vacuum seal them.

Stuffing is a natural accompaniment for your mashed potatoes and will mix nicely with spices and dehydrated onions.

Canned Fruits

Fruits contain twice as many calories per pound as veggies.

- A fruit cocktail will give you about 300-400 calories per pound. Fruit packed in a light syrup offers a tremendous calorie boost to aid you in survival. The liquids also provide a valuable source of hydration. Look for citrus varieties, such as pineapple and mandarin oranges, for essential vitamin C.

- Applesauce can be a wonderful accompaniment to cereals and can be served as a dessert or a snack.
- Canned pumpkin puree will also provide a heavy dose of Vitamin A and you can make a simple soup by adding bouillon cubes and spices, such as garlic.

Canned Liquids

It is important to stock up on canned foods with high liquid content. Two excellent (and often overlooked) examples are canned pineapples or canned pineapple juice and vegetable juice. These foods will provide nutrition and hydration simultaneously. Consider evaporated milk, condensed milk, and canned coconut milk. Coconut milk will help you cook rice faster. Stewed tomatoes and vegetables, beef, or chicken stock can also help you cook rice without depleting your drinking water. And here is a great rationale to stock up on beer; you can use it to cook, or even better, drink the beer.

Canned Meat

Purchase canned and dried meat, poultry, and fish for your pantry (think spam, tuna fish, etc.). Meat is the best prepper protein and with so many options available from dried and dehydrated, freeze-dried canned meats, you have no excuse. I dehydrate poultry, fish, and meats and store them in vacuum-sealed bags.

Canned Veggies

When it comes to veggies, preppers need to think beyond green beans. Unfortunately, green beans do not pack many calories. If you are looking for the ideal veggies to stock, then think about canned root vegetables, like sweet potatoes and yams. Sweet potatoes are high in vitamin A, and they are filling. Carrots, peas, and potatoes provide the fixing for a nice stew.

Canned olives, asparagus, and artichoke hearts will help you make easy pasta dishes.

Chocolates

Chocolate syrups and cocoa powders will serve you well in your food storage. Store a little chocolate, but not too much. Chocolate chips store relatively well. Remember also, baking chocolate. Not only does chocolate pack loads of antioxidants, but it is also a morale booster that could prove essential. Besides, chocolate (a food group) has been known to boost heart health.

Pack high-quality dark chocolate. If you look closely at the ingredients of other chocolates, like Hershey's Kisses, you will find an unwanted ingredient: hydrogenated oils. Those do not belong in your chocolate, even during survival times.

Add chocolate chips to pancakes, muffins, cake, and more to delight kids and help keep the normalcy as best you can in a disaster situation.

Cereals

Stockpile whatever cereals your family eats: oat, corn, rice, or wheat-based. If refrigeration is not an issue, stock wheat germ, which has high levels of fiber and vitamin E to boost your immune system.

Wheat germ is the center of the seed. Packed with protein and fiber, wheat germ also has folate, magnesium, zinc, manganese, selenium, and vitamin

E. It is considered nutrition when one is in a tight spot. It is not a meal, but one you can add to your hot cereal.

Condiments

Your favorite condiments will go a long way toward making foods taste better in uncertain times. Here is a list of some of my favorites.

- Pickle
- Relish
- Whole Grain Mustard
- Mayonnaise
- Ketchup
- Tabasco sauce
- Liquid Aminos (liquid amino acids)
- Worcestershire sauce

Corn as a Grain

Corn is both a grain and a vegetable. As a grain, corn is dried into flour to bake and make a variety of foods from cornbread to cornflakes. Corn as grain is an essential prepper food and there are many kinds of dried corn.

- Cornmeal
- Corn starch
- Grits
- Popcorn
- Dough

Corn as a Vegetable

Corn as a vegetable is also an important pantry essential; the only difference is that as a grain it is dried before harvesting.

Crackers and Cookies

While crackers have little nutritive value, they do provide a sense of normalcy to a survival situation and will be a worthy and satisfying accompaniment to soups, tuna salad, and peanut butter.

Distilled Water and Seltzer Water

Water is not a food, but you certainly cannot live without it, which is why water is #1 on all preppers' lists. Distilled water is the purest form of water. Get water now and make plans to get more water. Consider adding bottled seltzer water to your pantry as well. Seltzer water lasts indefinitely, adds a fizzy pep to your water supply, and even helps relieve constipation. Avoid seltzer if you have acid reflux.

Drink Mixes

Stock your prepper's pantry with drink mixes

- Coffee for survival purposes provides the benefit of increased mental alertness and boosts morale.
- Tea for survival is important and has been around for many millennia for a reason. The water quality of our ancestors was not very good, so tea helped it taste better and boiling water killed bacteria. In an emergency, tea can help you hydrate quickly when you cannot wait

for the boiled water to cool. Caffeinated teas provide a burst of additional energy, while other teas can provide a calming and soothing effect, which you may need. Consider including Echinacea, peppermint, and chamomile teas to help combat the common cold, naturally.

- Powdered drink mixes
    - Tang is a prepper classic to enhance the water supply. It has calcium and vitamin C to help avoid scurvy.
    - Gatorade powder provides a boost of electrolytes.
    - Kool-Aid or whatever tickles your sweet tooth.
    - Lemonade
- Bouillon cubes are compressed stock. This salty essential will help you flavor soups, rice, ramen style noodles, and gravies. Be careful since they are high in sodium and will cause you to drink more water.

Hard Cheese Encased in Wax

Waxed hard cheeses are not easy to find, but they are available. You will easily find parmesan, Swiss, sharp cheddar, or gouda packaged in this way. The wax prevents the cheese from growing mold and bacteria, and it keeps moisture in your cheese, so it can store for a long time without refrigeration. Parmesan is a hard cheese, and in the powder form has a four-month expiration date, but encased in wax it can last up to twenty-five years. Consider buying cheese wax and even a basic hard cheese waxing kit to make your delicious cheeses.

Honey

Even if you do not use honey, buy some. Not only will it last forever, but also you will use it in survival times to flavor boring oatmeal and other breakfast grains, as well as teas. Honey eases sore throats, and more importantly, if you do not have any topical antibiotics, you can use honey as a paste to put on wounds. There are additional medicinal and other reasons to stock honey in your supplies.

I dedicate a whole chapter just for honey.

Jams and Jellies

Preppers love to make their jams and jellies, but if you are new to prepping, you can stock up on ready-made varieties. Jams and jellies are a canning favorite and include blackberry jams, strawberry jams, raspberry jams, grape jellies, and apple butter. Your pantry can have a variety of fruit spreads to sweeten life.

Leavening Agents

Both baking soda and baking powder are leavening agents, which means they produce carbon dioxide to help food rise.

- **Baking soda**. When you combine baking soda (sodium bicarbonate) with honey or an acidic ingredient like buttermilk or yogurt, you get a chemical reaction of carbon dioxide bubbles. This causes baked goods to rise. Baking soda can last about two years.
- **Baking powder**. Baking powder has sodium bicarbonate as an ingredient, along with an acidifying agent (cream of tartar for example) and a drying agent (such as starch). Baking powder lasts around a year and a half.

- **Dry yeast**. Unfortunately, yeast has a very short shelf life, but dry yeast is still well worth having on hand. Dry yeast is an essential leavening agent in baking bread and has a longer shelf life than compressed yeast, but still, after several months, it loses potency.

MREs

There are two kinds of shelf-stable, ready to eat meals: the kind you can eat, and the kind you cannot tolerate. Often they come with soup, which is good and can provide a hearty meal with some crackers.

For shelf-stable and ready to eat meals, think about adding canned meat to boxed meals.

In uncertain times, you can also take comfort in having several shelf-stable, ready to eat meals on hand, which require no cooking.

Nuts, Seeds, and Nut-Butters

Many preppers stock peanut butter, but sun butter, made from sunflower seeds, is an excellent item to stock, as is almond butter.

While it is true that nuts can go rancid quickly, nuts are an excellent source of energy, so stock up. Just be sure to rotate your stock often.

- Raw almonds, walnuts, and cashews are excellent choices, as well as pistachios.
- Mixed roasted nuts, such as hazelnuts, pecans, and Brazil nuts, will also provide a variety.
- Sunflower seeds and alfalfa seeds
- Try trail mixes and nut bars

Nuts are allergens, so avoid giving them to young children or anyone you suspect may be allergic.

Canned chestnuts are a great source of fiber. They are also an excellent source of potassium, magnesium, iron, and vitamin C. The healthiest nuts and seeds are in bags, rather than oil-filled cans and jars.

Make sure to stock peanut butter. Look for peanut butter that is simply peanuts, oil, and salt. Skip the peanut butter that has sugars in them or worse yet, those with hydrogenated oils. Know that "trans-fat-free" does not mean that they are free from trans-fats, it could mean that there is less than 0.05 grams of trans-fat per serving. Alternatively, you could make peanut butter. It is not difficult.

Oats and Oatmeal

Oatmeal is a prepper food that is low in saturated fat and a good source of fiber, which is especially important during survival times. You will need to store adequate water as making the porridge requires about a cup and a half of water for every one cup of oatmeal. A preparation tip is to soak the oatmeal overnight so that it takes about ten minutes to cook (instead of half an hour) or use an Instapot. Stock up on buckets of rolled oats and quick oats.

Oils

Cooking oil is extremely important to stockpile. You cannot cook much without oil or fat. Buy oil in small containers and look for the word "virgin" which means that they are the first press and have the most nutritive value. Cooking oil will not last long, but even if your oil becomes rancid, you can use it as fuel.

- **Butter**. You can freeze butter and buy butter in a can. Look also into butter powder.

- **Coconut oil**. Shortening usually has trans-fats, so consider coconut oil as cooking lard to replace Crisco or another vegetable shortening, which is made of dangerous trans-fats. Coconut oil is heat stable, and because it is slow to oxidize, it means that it will not go rancid as quickly as other oils. It can last up to two years, and it provides fast energy.
- **Sesame Oil**. Adds a unique flavor to your foods.
- **Ghee**. Ghee is butter that has been melted and simmered down until all the water has evaporated and the milk solids have settled at the bottom. It has a long shelf life.
- **Olive oil**. Olive oil is an ideal oil but can quickly go rancid, though it may have a shelf life up to two years.
- **Organic shortening**. Many preppers stock Crisco, which is not organic, but it is better to make a candle from Crisco than it is to eat the artery-clogging stuff. Organic shortening is a good alternative to hydrogenated Crisco because it is made healthier and it lasts indefinitely.
- **Other oils**. Whatever oil you buy, be sure to buy them in small containers as the minute you open them, they begin to oxidize and deteriorate quickly.

Pasta

Dried pasta is an ideal prep because it has little to no fat or moisture content, so it resists spoilage. Among the most filling and inexpensive foods, you should store a variety of pasta in addition to spaghetti and macaroni noodles – including egg noodles, gnocchi (made with potatoes), dried tortellini (filled with hard cheese), orzo (rice-shaped pasta), couscous (wheat-based pasta) and other varieties of shaped Italian pasta.

Potato Flakes

Potato flakes to make mashed potatoes are a wonderful addition to your pantry. They also have many other uses, including thickening of soups and stews. They help add more normalcy to your survival situation.

Potato Flour

Potato flour might not be at the top of your list but is good to have in your pantry. It is a wonderful, gluten-free addition to the pantry to make bread, pancakes and waffles, potato soups, and much more.

- It is a better way to eat your veggies. Potato flour is the entire potato, including the skin, dehydrated.
- You can use potato flour as a thickener to add body to broths, stews, and gravies. It is the starch in the potato that holds water.
- It is a natural dough conditioner. As a baking ingredient to mix with other flours, potato flour will add moisture. Potato flour makes yeast dough easier to handle.
- Used as a binder, potato flour will add creaminess to frozen desserts because it holds the moisture and the fat. It also helps bind meats such as hamburger patties, meatloaf, or fish patties, so they are juicier and more flavorful.
- Potato flour is a gluten-free breading for frying. It provides a golden crunchy crust.

- Potato flour will add shelf life to foods you bake because it is a moist yeast bread.

Also consider sweet potato flour, which is incredibly versatile and can be used for baked goods such as bread, cookies, muffins, pancakes, crepes, cakes, and doughnuts. It can also be used in soups, as a thickener for sauces, and gravies, and breading.

Powdered Milk, Whey, and Eggs

Powdered milk will come in handy for many things. I devote an entire chapter to milk and powdered milk

Milk is a versatile food well worth stockpiling if you do not have a cow or a goat. Whole milk powder will last up to two years (or more if stored properly) and is an excellent natural creamer for coffee. Skip the non-dairy creamers made of hydrogenated oils and use powdered milk instead.

- Powdered milk is an excellent source of calcium and tastes just like milk.
- In cheese making, curds are the thick part of the milk that is separated from the liquid when the milk turns sour. Whey is the watery part that is cloudy and yellowish. Whey is highly nutritious and contains all the essential amino acids required by the body for strength and muscle development. It is a great way of increasing protein intake without adding excessive carbohydrates and fat. It dissolves instantly so it is great for making high protein shakes and smoothies. In survival times, mix it with dehydrated milk for an extra frothy and satisfying source of nutrients.
- Eggs generally last about two months and need to be refrigerated. However, having egg powders on hand is peace of mind.

Protein Bars and Drinks

Ideal for a bug out bag, food bars are compact nutrition and should be part of your everyday food storage. High in protein, serve them for breakfast, snacks, desserts, or as an on-the-go meal replacement. Skip the granola bars, which will crack your teeth and are generally high in sugar.

Raisins and Dried Fruits

Enhance your supply with dried apricots, dates, cranberries, mangos, and whatever your family enjoys. You can make your trail mix with dried fruits. You can dehydrate the fruits yourself and mix and match to your tastes.

- **Raisins**. Just a handful of raisins will provide a full serving of fruit. Raisins have protein, fiber, iron, and vitamin C. Raisins are loaded with antioxidants and potassium. Use them to enhance the flavor of rice for dinner and cereals for breakfasts. Remember, raisins are dried fruit and not dehydrated food. There is a difference in how you store each.
    - Dried fruit should be packed loosely into an airtight glass or plastic container. This allows any remaining moisture to distribute evenly among the fruit slices. If condensation forms, the fruit is not sufficiently dried and should be dehydrated further. Store packaged dehydrated fruit from the garden in a cool, dark area to help it retain the vitamin content of the fruit. Dried fruit can also be stored in the freezer or

refrigerator which will help to extend its shelf life.

- Most dehydrated foods can be stored in a vacuum-sealed container or bag for many years.

- **Fruit leathers, fruit strips, and fruit ropes**. Skip the fruit rollups, which are laden with unwanted high-fructose corn syrups. Instead, look for fruit twists and high fiber dried fruit strips available in a variety of flavors, such as cherry, grape, and apricot, and fruit ropes.

The more variety you have on hand, the better for your family to fight boredom in their diet and to get the essential nutrients each provides.

Rice

Rice is a staple of the prepper diet (along with beans). Sure, Jasmine rice is cheap food, and worth storing but you can have a variety on hand to keep your family interested. Try basmati rice, short-grain Asian rice, wild rice, and brown rice too. Brown rice is a healthy option but requires more cooking time, which could deplete your cooking resources. It also does not store as well. Consider instant rice for this reason alone, though it is not as healthy as other rice options.

Salt

There are many reasons to stockpile salt. Look to history and you will find salt was an important commodity used for a variety of purposes (including as money: the word "salary" derives from the Latin word for salt). Salt can kill bacteria and contains chloride and sodium ions and all living things need these components in small quantities. Not all salt is the same. Humans need iodized salt to avoid thyroid gland problems and goiter and to help regulate fluid balance in the body.

We also need salt to preserve food. Salt inhibits the growth of germs in a process of osmosis where the salt pushes the water out of the microbial cells. Best of all, salt lasts forever. You can salt everything from salad greens to curing meats and preserving other kinds of food. Indeed, salt is very useful to preppers and I talk more about it later in a chapter dedicated to it.

Spices and Herbs

Spices will sure make that boring rice tastier, and chili peppers add flavor to all those beans you are storing. Buy more of the spices already in your cupboard. Some good basics include dill, red pepper, cumin, rosemary, garlic, oregano, dried mustard, and ginger in addition to the saffron and chili. Skip the strong spices like curry. While it tastes wonderful, it may also attract human predators.

Sugar and Molasses

I recommend stocking up on cane sugar, brown sugar, and powdered sugar for your baking needs. I also suggest skipping the beet sugar and buying cane sugar in the raw. Buy sugar and wrap it in plastic, because this helps protect it from insects. As a second step, you can buy sugars and then place your sugar into Mylar bags and food-grade plastic buckets sealed with a gamma lid. Look for sugar in the raw packets.

Check out the chapter on sugar, later on.

Vanilla Extract

Vanilla extract is a common ingredient in baking; some might even say it is the most important of flavors. I also use it in cooking some dishes (for example, French toast).

Vitamins

Staying at peek vitality is crucial during episodes of stress. While multi-vitamins are a great idea, be sure to pack calcium fortified with vitamin D, as this combination may help your body fight infections. Also, look for magnesium; as an essential stress supplement, magnesium prevents the damage caused by excess adrenaline.

Do not forget to stock up on vitamins specifically for your children.

Vodka

Vodka is on the prepper list of morale-boosting foods. You can cook with vodka or drink it. Vodka has some medicinal value. Use vodka as a mouthwash or help numb the pain of a toothache. Apply vodka on a cotton ball or a Q-tip and dab on cold sores to dry them out, as an anesthetic for blisters, or to ease poison ivy and as a skin repellent to shoo flies and mosquitoes. Wipe bad smells away with vodka. Try vodka too for cleaning the lenses of eyeglasses.

It is also great for barter.

Whole Wheat Flour, Bread, and Pancake Mixes

Bread mixes fall into the category of flour. Wheat is a basic food product that is full of fiber, protein, vitamins, and minerals, such as selenium. If you stock white flour in your daily pantry, be sure to stock whole-wheat flour as well because it has more nutritive value when it has the whole grain (bran, germ, and endosperm). White flour has only the endosperm.

When purchasing flour, do NOT get bleached flour. Why would you want to put bleach into your body?

You may also use flour for thickening gravies, or to coat and fry, such things as freshly caught fish.

Ultimately, you should store whole-wheat flour in your everyday pantry. Your long-term pantry should include whole-grain wheat and you should consider a grain mill.

Wine

Make your wine or buy it, but having wine will be indispensable. I recommend raisin wine or dandelion wine. At the least, you can use it for barter and I use it for cooking.

Just for the fun of it, I include my recipe for raisin wine.

Raisin Wine Recipe

2 gallons of water
2 pounds of raisins
4 to 5 pounds of sugar

Mix all ingredients and let sit for about four to six weeks. Stir once every other day.

MILK

Stocking powdered and dehydrated milk in your emergency pantry is important for body and mind. With powdered milk, you can make yogurt, sour cream, cream cheese, buttermilk, and more.

From beverages, bread, dips and spreads, soups, to sauces, powdered milk is a staple to stockpile.

Calcium & Vitamin D

Many people drink milk for strong bones. Milk is a good source of calcium and vitamin D. Calcium and vitamin D work together to strengthen your bones and teeth. Vitamin D has a role in the absorption of both calcium and phosphorus. Vitamin D is known to help the brain and memory.

Vitamins

Powdered milk packs a variety of vitamins to help you get through stressful times. In addition to vitamin D and calcium, milk has vitamins A, B, C, and E.

- **Vitamin A**. A cup of milk has about ten percent of the daily requirement of vitamin A. Both adults and kids need vitamin A for good vision and immune health, as well as for the healthy development and maintenance of body tissues.
- **Vitamin B**. Vitamin B is responsible for energy production and helps maintain healthy nerves and red blood cells, as well as normal cell division.
- **Vitamin C**. Milk makes a small contribution to the body's vitamin C requirements, but in an emergency, every little bit counts.
- **Vitamin E**. It is great for the skin, helps to prevent cell damage (antioxidant), and reduces the risk of certain cancers.
- **Iodine**. Milk is a major contributor of iodine, which is vital to life.

Potassium

Potassium is a mineral (not a vitamin). If you have ever had a cramp in your leg, the cause is likely a lack of potassium. The lack of potassium can lead to high blood pressure.

Protein

Milk is a good source of protein.

Make Creamy Sauces and Gravies

With powdered milk and your whisk, you can whip up creamy sauces for pasta or gravies for meats and stews.

Coffee, Tea, and Cocoa

You will never run out of creamer when you have enough powdered milk. Adding powdered milk to your pantry will ensure a creamy cup of your favorite hot beverage.

Make Cheese

Another incredible thing you can do with the right ingredients in your food storage is to make a farmer's style cheese from powdered milk.

Camping

Not just for emergencies, powdered milk is also perfect for use during camping trips or to enhance your water in a bugout situation. Powdered milk used to have a funny taste, but that has changed in the recent past. It is delicious and you have many options.

Cereal

Cereal is another reason why you will want to stockpile milk. As a prepper, you likely have cereal and granola in your food storage and unless you want to eat these dry, you should stash some milk. Oatmeal and creamed wheat are much better and creamier with milk.

Cookies

Satisfying your soul by dipping a cookie in milk will evoke positive memories of your childhood.

Milk Prices Rise During Droughts

Both meat and dairy prices tend to rise as the livestock feed shortfalls caused by droughts occur.

HONEY

Preppers will especially appreciate the survival and medicinal uses of honey. Below are some of the benefits of honey so you will know how to use it in a survival situation.

Benefits

Honey has antibacterial activity. It also tastes good and lasts forever.

- **Antibiotic activity**. Honey is an antimicrobial, inhibiting the growth of bacteria. Instead of reaching for the Neosporin, reach for honey to put on your cuts, scrapes, and burns.

Does Not Expire

Honey is a shelf-stable survival food and medicine that can outlast you. Honey changes slightly over time, but it remains edible and does not spoil. One of the main reasons honey does not expire is because it lacks water. Microorganisms cannot survive in such low moisture environments.

Topical Medicinal Remedy

One of the primary survival and medicinal uses of honey is an antibacterial dressing. Honey is a mild acid that limits bacterial growth making it the ideal barrier against infection.

- **Heal cuts with honey**. Help your wounds heal faster with honey. Dressings can be used in all phases of wound healing. Just put some honey on a gauze pad and apply it to the wound.
- **Calm irritated skin**. Honey calms irritated skin as a topical treatment to help reduce itchiness and redness that can be associated with eczema, dermatitis, and extremely dry skin.
- **Ease a burn**. Topically applied, honey provides a nutritive element to your skin and can decrease inflammation, making it an ideal remedy for burns.
- **Dab honey on your lips**. Honey is a wonderful natural moisturizer and lip balm. If you are out of lip balm, reach for your tasty honey.
- **Take the bite out**. Honey calms and reduces swelling caused by mosquito or insect bites and stings.
- **Honey is a natural for dressings**. Whisk a little honey and apple cider vinegar with some olive oil and put that on a gauze pad.

Oral Medicinal Remedy

Honey is a medicine you can eat. Because it contains antibacterial and anti-inflammatory properties to fight against infections, you can use honey medicinally in many ways from sore throats to nausea and allergies. Below are some ways to use honey as medicine.

- **Soothe a sore throat with honey**. Heal a sore throat with honey by infusing honey with lemon in hot water as a tea. If you have it, add a little ginger.
- **Calm a cough with honey.** A spoonful of honey is cough medicine. It may be an old wives' tale, but as a cough suppression, honey may reduce phlegm. Take one or two teaspoons of honey with cinnamon at bedtime. Honey calms inflamed membranes helping to substantiate the claim that honey assists with a cold.
- **Relieve nausea with honey**. Honey can help in two ways to relieve nausea:
    - **Honey is a hangover helper**. Honey provides a remedy for a hangover. Loaded with natural fructose, honey speeds the metabolism of alcohol.
    - **It helps ease morning sickness**. Mix honey with ginger and lemon to create an elixir that should help relieve nausea associated with pregnancy.
- **Alleviate allergies**. A cup of tea infused with honey can do wonders for relieving your allergies, especially if you get raw honey that is locally farmed.

Nurture Your Skin

Another way honey can help you in your preps is as a facial cleanser and moisturizer. While you can buy commercial products with honey as a featured ingredient, you can use honey directly on your skin.

Adds Flavor

Fight boredom in the bunker with honey, which adds flavor to your foods in some surprising ways. Honey is a great choice for cornbread and granola. It is also an excellent natural sweetener for plain yogurt. What follows are some suggestions.

- Add honey to your oatmeal and other breakfast grains.
- Granola bars
- Honey as syrup is also delicious on pancakes, especially with butter.
- Try honey and lime or honey and soy sauce for two distinctly different honey meat glazes.
- Bake honey into bread and dinner rolls.
- Pair pretzels with honey for a sweet and salty taste you will start to crave. If you put the pretzels in the fridge overnight and allow the honey to coagulate as a coating, then you are in for an extra special treat.
- Add butter to your honey (equal parts of butter and honey) for a wonderful spread.
- Add honey to your teas and smoothies.
- Honey is better for you than refined sugars.
- Honeycomb is also edible if you are lucky enough to have a hive. You can find the honeycomb in some stores.

Immune System Booster

Honey also supports the proper functioning of your immune system.

Energy Booster

Get an energy lift from honey. Nature's secret is a mix of enzymes, amino acids, and antioxidants Honey can help you with survival by giving you more energy. It also packs carbohydrates, but raw honey, in particular, has a high nutritive value, and provides a natural energy boost, like sugar.

It seems odd that honey is an energy booster when we tell you that honey can help you sleep.

Sleep Aid

Think of honey as nature's energy booster for more restful sleep. Your body needs the energy to rebuild cells.

Honey is a helpful resource as a sleep aid depending on how you use it. Here are two excellent ways to help you catch some sleep time.

- Pair honey with an herbal tea for a calming effect. Honey has soothing properties that you can draw out with some herbal tea.
- Sleep like a baby with this age-old remedy of honey milk:
    - 6 oz. warm milk
    - 1 drop vanilla extract
    - 1 teaspoon honey

Allergies

Honey may help relieve allergies as well. On the theory that honey acts as a sort of vaccine or immune therapy as it has small doses of local pollen in it. Over time, the pollen sensitivity you might have had will dissipate as you build immunity to the allergens.

The catch is the honey must be local and raw, and you must consume a spoonful a day to help build your immunity to allergens.

Preservative

In its original state, honey is a preservative. Think of using honey to help you preserve your dehydrated fruits and even for preserves. Fruits immersed in honey are less prone to spoilage. This is because the moisture content in honey is very low. If you dehydrate fruits such as apples, apricots or bananas, then try pre-treating fruit with honey as a preservative before drying.

SUGAR

Most experts agree that for optimum health you should avoid sugar; however, there are some major misconceptions about this basic ingredient in part because the definition of sugar has been lumped into one category. Natural sugar has been getting an unfairly bad rap because it is being confused with synthetic sugars.

Not So Bad

Sugar provides energy and sustenance and offers a host of benefits. Your brain requires sugar (glucose) to function. Some sugars are vital to your health.

Sugar is not as bad as the media would have you think, but Americans are consuming too much of the wrong kind of sugar (processed fructose), because food manufacturers have been sneaking bad sugars into American food, and now the media is generalizing that all sugars are bad for your health.

There are good sugars, bad sugars, and ugly sugars. I will try to dissect the information for you to make it somewhat easier to understand and make your own decisions and choices.

- **Good.** One-hundred percent pure cane sugar, unbleached, organic. Raw cane sugar is healthy and alkaline. Cane sugar is best in the unbleached state and is not cut with beet sugars. Look for organic sugar, such as pure cane sugar or raw cane sugar that is minimally refined.
- **Bad.** White granulated sugar, beet sugar, and agave. If your sugar just says "sugar" then likely it is beet sugar. Generally, all beet sugar is GMO and chemically processed. From plant to the table, corn-derived and beet sugars go through an entirely different process than raw cane sugar. Both corn-derived and beet sugar start as a genetically modified product. Processed fructose is the worst sugar possible: it is also referred to as high fructose corn syrup. Another surprise is agave which is bad not only due to the concentration of fructose but because it is created in a highly chemical process.
- **Ugly.** Processed fructose – all corn-derived, and artificial sugars. Corn derived sugars are the ugliest of all sugars for your health, specifically high fructose corn syrup being the evilest since this is artificially derived is the most prevalent sugar substitute on the market. Finally, the artificial sugars, including aspartame and saccharine are the ugly stepsisters to processed fructose.

SUGAR

The worst sugar of all is high fructose corn syrup because it is an artificially produced chemical that quickly metabolizes into fat. America's obesity problem is entwined with the quick artificial boost from high fructose corn syrup. Become a label reader and throw away everything in your cabinets that has high fructose corn syrup.

Replace what you can with organic cane sugars or pure cane sugars.

Start stockpiling the right kind of sugar. Cane sugar earns an honorable place in prepping as it can heal, preserve food, boost morale, give energy, and more.

Energy

Cane sugar is fuel. Proof positive is that it burns easily when exposed to flame. Not that you needed any convincing that sugar is fuel, but it is interesting to note that sugar cane processing plants use sugar cane stalk residue, called bagasse, as fuel to run the cane factory. Sugar cane has a future as a renewable energy source. It fuels both the body and some mechanical machinery.

Every living creature runs off the simple sugar we call glucose.

Hydration

Sugar mixed with salt and water is an electrolyte. It is medicine all on its own and can help cure diarrhea. Essentially, sugar helps fluids leave your gut more rapidly, so it assists with hydration.

Normally the large intestine soaks up extra water, but when they do not; your body gets rid of the extra fluid through diarrhea. To restore the body, it is important to balance water and electrolytes and you can do this with a home remedy. A simple mixture of salt, sugar, and water is an electrolyte solution that can help you in many ways.

Raw cane sugar is energizing and thirst-quenching. That is because raw sugar cane juice contains organic salts and vitamins. Best of all, raw sugar cane juice is good for diabetes patients.

Canning Jams and Jellies

Sugar helps the canning process with color retention, gelling, and preserving in jams and jellies.

- As sugar readily absorbs water, it prevents the fruit from absorbing water, which would otherwise cause the color of your fruits to fade.
- Sugar is essential in the gelling process and pectin can form this gel only with sugar and acid. The sugar attracts and holds the water during the gelling process. Gelling depends on the acidity and some recipes achieve proper levels through lemon juice or citric acid. Also, the ratio of sugar depends on the desired consistency and the amount of pectin in the fruit, which varies with ripeness. In perfect combination, the gel-forming process of gelation happens with fruit, sugar, and acid.
- Sugar protects canned jams, jellies, and preserves from spoilage due to bacteria and yeast until the lid is opened and the product is exposed to air. After the lid opens, sugar continues the job of attracting water to incapacitate any microorganisms.

Baked Goods

Preppers will want to store sugar because it is an essential ingredient in recipes, particularly baked goods, such as cornbread. Sugar interacts with protein molecules and/or starch in the baking process. As a leavening agent, sugar increases the effectiveness of yeast. If you have ever wondered why many loaves of bread contain sugar, it is because of fermentation. The sugar is food for the yeast to rise.

- Sugar aids in creaming to promote lightness.
- Sugar serves as a whipping aid to stabilize beaten eggs.

Meat Tenderizer

Sugar can act as a meat tenderizer by absorbing water and helping with the texture. Sugar interacts with molecules of protein or starch in the baking and cooking process.

Fermentation

If you want to make wine or beer, you will need sugar. The sugar feeds the yeast to make fermented beverages.

- Winemakers convert fruit sugars into alcohol by a fermentation process. Sometimes fruit sugar is low and winemakers add sugar in a process called chaptalization.
- Beer makers, or brewers, add priming sugar when bottling the beer, so the yeast has something to eat which in turn produces carbonation. Fermented sugars are extracted from malted barley (mostly maltose); yeast

assists in removing the complex sugars from the grain.

Diabetics

To some, sugar is the villain, but for diabetics, it can have its advantages. First, it is significant to note that eating sugar has nothing to do with developing Type I diabetes. Type I diabetes has everything to do with genetics. The true cause of Type II diabetes is obesity.

Sugar is important to diabetics for many reasons. Cane sugar can heal skin ulcers and surprisingly even help heal diabetes.

If you have either Type I or Type II diabetes, please follow your doctor's orders.

Morale Booster

It is no secret that sugar just makes food taste better and that kids (of all ages) love it. Given that sugar provides a sense of normalcy in a crisis, it is a good idea to stockpile it.

Lasts Indefinitely

As long as the critters do not get into your sugar, you will be fine for twenty-five years or more.

SALT

Most people do not give salt a second thought. They have some in the cupboard and there it sits until dinnertime. Some people do all they can to avoid it, but salt is vital to survival and an important part of prepping.

Today it is quite inexpensive and as a prepper, you should not only stock up but store it properly.

Salt not only balances electrolytes that regulate your heart rate and ensures proper cell function, it can also treat a variety of ailments. Salt can assist when there is no doctor to treat sore throats nor dentist to ease tooth pain. As well, salt can help preppers make soap, clean up around the homestead and to preserve food. Most importantly, salt can make bland food taste better.

Storing Salt

Storing salt for the long term is vital and easy. Salt never goes bad. As with many things, keep salt in a cool and dark place.

How Much

I have heard that one should store anywhere between three to ten pounds per person per year. I tend to gravitate toward the higher number. I would rather have too much than too little and any extra is good for bartering.

Types of Salt

There are many kinds of salts for survival, and each one has its specific purpose and use.

- Canning and pickling salts
- Iodized salt
- Non-iodized salt
- Epsom salt (not for eating)
- Pink Himalayan salt
- Sea salt and Celtic sea salt
- Salt licks for livestock
- Popcorn salt

Electrolyte Balance

Salt is important for your body for water retention and electrolyte balance. Electrolytes are in your blood, urine, and other body fluids: electrolytes, among other functions, help with muscle contraction. Salt also has minerals vital to digestion. When the stuff hits the fan, you will need salt for electrolyte balance.

Food Preservation

One of the most important reasons to store salt is food preservation.

From salt cures to pickling and preserves, it is immensely useful as a food preservative. Salt preserves food by inhibiting the growth of germs in a process of osmosis where the salt effectively pushes the water out of the microbial cells thereby inactivating them.

Extinguish a Fire

As a fire extinguisher, salt is invaluable with grease fires. As you may know, water will only make a grease fire worse. Dousing salt on it can help you to effectively smother the flames.

Fireplace Cleanup

Salt is valuable for extinguishing a fire, but you can also use it to clean up a fireplace. Salt helps with creosote buildup. Creosote forms when warm air leaves the flue and the heavy cool air gets to the bottom of a wood burner. When you douse the flames with salt, your fire will burn out quickly. This means you will have less soot than if you let it smolder.

Spread a cup of table salt on the coals or logs every week of use and it will cause the creosote buildup to flake off.

Bartering

Salt is an easy-to-store and inexpensive bartering item that would serve a prepper well in a long-term survival scenario.

Make sure to transfer the salt to watertight containers, such as Mason jars, food-grade buckets, Mylar bags, and the like. You do not want moisture to degrade your salt in storage or have it wash away.

Disinfectant

Salt is a natural cleaning agent and abrasive. Rub cutting boards with salt and a damp cloth to improve the appearance after washing them in soap and water.

Pest Control

Salt is excellent for pest control. Salt drives away ants and kills slugs.

Thawing and Melting Ice

Salt will certainly help clear icy roads, driveways, and walkways.

Attracting Wild Game

Every living thing needs salt. Use salt not only for your livestock but also set out salt licks to attract wild game.

The Himalayan rock salt lick is filled with essential vitamins and minerals that animals both crave and need.

Types of Salt

There are many forms of salt and each variety has its uses. Stock as many types as you think you will need.

SALT

- **Sea salt**. Natural sea salt does not have iodine.
- **Iodized salt**. Iodized salt is essential for humans. Humans need iodized salt to avoid thyroid gland problems and goiter and to help regulate fluid balance in the body.
- **Pickling salt**. Preppers will need pickling salt to brine. Pickling salt has no iodine in it because iodine oxidizes food and darkens it.
- **Meat tenderizing salts**. Morton Curing Salts are perfectly formulated.
    - The **Plain Sugar Cure Mix** is for dry or sweet pickle curing of meat, game, poultry, salmon, and other fish.
    - The **Smoke Flavored** variety is great for large cuts of meat like bacon and hams. Only for dry curing, not for making a pickling brine.
    - The **Tender Quick** is a fast cure product used on meats, game, poultry, salmon, and other fish. Use as a dry cure or a pickling cure.
- **Kosher salt**. The craggy crystals of kosher salt make it perfect for curing meat. Kosher salt is a chef's favorite because it dissolves quickly and disperses flavors evenly.
- **Himalayan salt** is a mineral-rich salt. Himalayan pink salt is a miraculous and beautiful unrefined salt that will heal you from the inside out.
- **Cattle Salt**. Ranchers need salt for their livestock; some are mixed in the trough, while others are used as salt blocks. Salt blocks can be used to attract wildlife.
- **Epsom salt**. Not an edible salt but it is a prepper's best friend. See the following chapter just on Epsom salt.

- **Popcorn salt**. A fine grain of salt that is good for popcorn as it adheres better especially when on buttered popcorn.

How to Find Salt

Salt is an important part of your diet and you may be wondering how to find salt in the wild. The answer is surprisingly simple: you will find salt in your food. Salt is a natural part of many foods including:

- Beans
- Peanuts
- Vegetables: beetroot, carrots, celery, chard, potatoes, spinach
- Meat
- Milk
- Seawater
- Seafood
- Tuna
- Mineral deposits
- Celery

EPSOM SALT

Epsom salt (magnesium sulfate) has earned its place in the prepper's medicine cabinet, and for good reason. Epsom salt can help relieve muscle aches and pains. It is also useful for growing tastier tomatoes, deterring slugs, warding off raccoons, and getting rid of splinters. Some other unexpected survival uses of Epsom salt include relief from the itch of mosquito bites, bee stings, and poison ivy – even the pain and itch of the shingles.

An old medicinal friend, Epsom salt, is making a comeback helping people who have a magnesium deficiency, those with heart problems and so much more. From stinky feet to dealing with annoying ants, Epsom salt is a miraculous substance.

Remember that Epsom salt is not edible and should only be used topically as a soak or a compress.

Epsom Salt in Prepping

With a history of helping to ease headaches, it can also help alleviate stress, and even energize you. Epsom salt is so much more than a foot soak.

Foot Care

The obvious and primary use of Epsom salt is as a foot soak. Your feet will take a beating in an off-grid life, and Epsom salt can help keep your feet ready for whatever emergency or homesteading task comes your way – it can even keep your feet ready to bug out and hit the trails. It provides relief for tired feet from too much standing or over-exertion, but it is helpful in many other ways.

- **Alleviating athlete's foot.** Athletes' foot can be a side effect of walking with bare feet in public gyms, showers, pools, and other public spaces. Mix Epsom salt with a few drops of tea tree oil[3] to soak away fungus and bacteria from the skin surface.
- **Treating toenail fungus.** Get rid of nasty toenail fungus with the aid of an Epsom salt foot soak with tea tree oil. A daily foot soak is important, as keeping your feet out of shoes and socks as much as possible until the condition is resolved. Wear sandals and enjoy a soak until the toenail fungus disappears.
- **Soaking** your feet in Epsom salt will also make nail cutting easier. Use it to help manage brittle nails. You can add drops of tea tree oil to

[3] An essential oil It is derived from the leaves of the tea tree, Melaleuca alternifolia, native to southeast Queensland and the northeast coast of New South Wales, Australia.

regular Epsom salt or buy one formulated with tea tree oil.

- **Foot smells.** The medical term for bad smelling feet is “Bromodosis”, and it is a common medical condition that comes from the buildup of sweat and bacteria. A soak in Epsom salt will get rid of foul-smelling feet. It can eliminate the odor, as well as itching, burning, and inflammation of your feet; for the stinky foot smell that collects in your footwear, you can sprinkle a little Epsom salt in your shoes and scrub away the stench.
- **Softening calluses.** Calluses happen when the outermost layer of skin on hands or feet suffers from repeated friction. You can soften calluses with a warm Epsom salt soak but remember that your body thickens the skin to help protect it. To prevent your skin from thickening again after an Epsom salt soak, be sure to use moleskin, get a new pair of shoes, or otherwise find a way to stop the friction that is causing the problem.
- **Healing your heel fissures.** “Heel fissures” are the cracks in the rough part of your heel, which are sometimes painful and may bleed. Deep cracks can become infected. To avoid heel fissures, soak in Epsom salt and use a pumice stone to smooth out the layers of skin, then top off your treatment with a moisturizer. Causes of heel fissures include diabetes, obesity, or living in an arid climate. It is particularly important for people who have compromised immune systems to treat fissures to avoid infections. In addition to an Epsom salt routine, be sure to moisturize feet twice daily. You can concentrate the moisture at night by wearing socks when asleep.

Regulate Blood Pressure

Epsom salt acts as a powerful detox as well as pain relief for your head, heart, and kidneys.

Magnesium is nature's secret medicine and Epsom salt will help you get more of it. It might surprise you to learn that magnesium is one as a key to regulating blood pressure.

You will need about two cups of Epsom salt per average size bathtub to reap the benefits. Just sprinkling some in the bathtub will do nothing.

Relieve a Headache

Magnesium is one option for migraine prevention that is also safe and effective.

Whether or not you take magnesium supplements, soaking in Epsom salt will help you relieve migraine headaches by allowing you to absorb more of that element, and simultaneously help flush toxins from your body.

Relieve Itchy Skin

Another reason preppers should stockpile Epsom Salt is that it is a cure-all for a variety of skin ailments. It provides a relaxing soak to soothe dry and itchy skin, control blemishes, and even help with the shingles.

- **Shingles**. Epsom salt can relieve pain from shingles and can increase circulation. Epsom salt will be a welcome relief to the painful, blistering skin rash of shingles from the varicella-zoster virus, which is the same virus that causes chickenpox – especially when the SHTF and there are no doctors around. To use it for the shingles, add two cups of Epsom salt to a soothing warm bath. If a bath is not possible, you can make a paste and apply it directly to the skin.

- **Eczema and psoriasis**. Alcohols and fragrances in the products you use can aggravate eczema, but thankfully, Epsom salt can provide relief. Flare-ups of psoriasis may be incurable, but you can get relief with Epsom salt as well.
- **Mosquito bites and bee stings**. Epsom salt has anti-inflammatory properties to alleviate swelling from bites and stings. To help relieve the itch of a mosquito bite or the pain of a bee sting, make an Epsom salt compress.
- **Sunburn and first-degree burns**. Another reason to make a compress is to soothe burned and damaged skin. A cool or lukewarm water soak of Epsom salt will help irrigate the wounds and the compress will extend the relief. You can make a small batch with a 1/4 cup of Epsom salt to a cup of water, then soak a soft cloth, wring and apply to the wound.
- **Poison ivy and poison oak**. A warm Epsom salt bath will provide immediate relief of the pain and itch of poison ivy or poison oak. Follow up the treatment with an Epsom salt compress to reduce inflammation.
- **Acne**. As a facial scrub or skin exfoliant, Epsom salt will help you treat acne to reduce inflammation and scarring.

Reduce Bruising

Epsom salt not only helps relieve minor sprains, sore muscle, and backaches; it makes bruises go away faster. Bruising that appears on the surface of your skin goes much deeper into muscle tissues than you may think. It is the damaged blood cells beneath the skin that collects near the surface of the skin that changes the color of your skin. Epsom salt relaxes muscles and reduces inflammation to reduce the appearance of bruising.

If you find a painful blood blister, soak your feet in two cups of Epsom salt in warm water.

Alleviate Leg Cramps

Epsom salt work wonders for leg cramps. A leg or muscle cramp is an often-painful contraction or tightening of a muscle that comes on suddenly. Leg cramps are caused by a lack of calcium, potassium, and other minerals, including magnesium. You can get relief from an Epsom salt soak or compress. Be sure to hydrate as well.

Relax Body and Mind

In times of crisis and stress, Epsom salt can help provide a sense of calm. Stress robs your body of magnesium, and Epsom salt can help restore and balance this deficiency. That is because Epsom salt is magnesium sulfate, which acts not only to calm inflammation but also as a sedative for the nervous system. Soaking your feet in a tub of warm water with Epsom salt will help restore vitality and get you back on your feet in no time.

Provided water is abundantly available, preppers can enjoy relaxing in a tub of water and Epsom salt to get relief from the workday.

Garden

You can use Epsom salt as a plant food supplement, fertilizer, and pest control agent.

EPSOM SALT

Epsom salt is great for potted plants and garden plants because it adds more sulfur into the soil. For generations, gardeners have used Epsom salt, and now preppers are taking notice and doing the same.

- **Fertilizes your plants**. Epsom salt is an excellent fertilizer for tomato plants but also helps peppers and other plants grow strong.
- **Remedies magnesium deficiencies in plants**. Just like humans, plants are often magnesium-deficient.
- **Keeps slugs at bay**. Get rid of annoying garden slugs because they hate salt. Using Epsom salt to deter slugs is an organic gardening technique that will simultaneously enhance the pH of your soil.

Household

Epsom salt has uses beyond the garden. Try using Epsom salt to clean the tiles of your bathroom and kitchen.

- **Bathroom**. The salts are a mild abrasive to get into the grout when you mix with dishwashing liquid. Cleaning your home with Epsom salt will help reduce your dependency on harmful chemicals.
- **Kitchen**. Try using Epsom salt on pots, pans, and dishes on which food was burned. Epsom salt helps you to get them clean.

Diabetes

Preppers with diabetes must take caution when using Epsom salt. Talk to your physician to see whether Epsom salt is right for you.

What makes Epsom salt promising is that it can help heal foot sores associated with diabetes, and help improves insulin levels. Unfortunately, Epsom salt can also dry skin on the toes and feet, add to uncontrolled fluctuations in blood sugar levels, and lower blood pressure too much. For most diabetics, frequent use is out of the question; however, for those in good control of glucose levels, and in good contact with a physician, occasional use may be a healthy option.

In short, Epsom salt draws toxins from the body, sedates the nervous system, reduces swelling, relaxes muscles, and is a natural emollient, exfoliator, and much more.

Laxative

Constipation is an overlooked prepper problem, due to a steady diet of beans, constipating MREs, and gut clogging freeze-dried foods. Epsom salt can help relieve constipation as a laxative if you do not have enough fiber in your diet. A food grade dietary supplement can help.

The use of Epsom salt adds magnesium through absorption. As mentioned above, stress robs you of magnesium; around fifty percent of Americans are magnesium deficient. Epsom salt can help to flush out toxins from the body, and thereby improve the absorption of nutrients. Specifically, through a foot soak absorption, Epsom salt can boost your magnesium levels.

With a history of easing headaches, alleviating stress, soothing aches, and pains, and even giving you more energy, remedy heart problems, and more, you will want to stock up on Epsom salt.

EPSOM SALT

Epsom salt has a variety of medicinal applications when topically applied; you can use Epsom salt as first aid for:

- Removing calluses
- Reducing swelling of sprains and bruises
- Easing gout
- Treating fungus in fingernails and toenails
- Relieving constipation (as a saline laxative Epsom salt can relieve occasional constipation and irregularity)
- Healing cuts and drawing out infections.
- Brushing teeth to help prevent periodontal disease

VINEGAR

Vinegar is essential to the prepper's pantry. Vinegar is the king of the prepper's cupboard, particularly apple cider vinegar. The ancients used vinegar recognizing its medicinal value and you should too.

Apple cider vinegar is generally made from crushed apples. Bacteria and yeast are added to ferment the liquid. At first, the liquid is similar to a hard apple cider because of the alcohol content. More fermentation changes the alcohol into vinegar (this is the same phenomenon that makes wines go sour).

Organic and raw apple cider vinegar are both allowed to ferment naturally. These liquids are unfiltered and typically take on a brownish, cloudy appearance. This process leaves behind the "mother" of the apple.

The mother is a cobweb-like substance found at the bottom of all bottles of organic apple cider vinegar. Non-organic apple cider vinegar is pasteurized, and the mother of apple is removed.

The mother is rich in enzymes, proteins, and pectin. Because of this, organic varieties are considered the gold standard when used to treat health conditions, such as acid reflux.

These statements have not been evaluated by the Food and Drug Administration. Nothing herein is intended to diagnose, treat, cure, or prevent any disease.

Helps Around the Kitchen

Apple cider vinegar is an exceptional product in the kitchen (and not just because it adds a tart flavor to your foods). Here are some interesting uses of apple cider vinegar around the kitchen.

- **Clean in an environmentally and budget-friendly way.** Vinegar is a safe bleach alternative for kitchen cleaning and has the benefit of being biodegradable. While vinegar is an acid and might not be suitable for all surfaces, it is certainly an inexpensive way to clean without chemicals. It works wonderfully to clean cutting boards and food preparation surfaces.
- **Unclog the kitchen sink.** In combination with baking soda, vinegar will create an effervescent scrubbing action that simultaneously deodorizes your kitchen sink and help it unclog.
- **Wash fruits and veggies**. Food contamination can cause gut problems. As a vegetable wash, vinegar will make your produce safe for consumption. It also gives a lift to wilted vegetables when you soak them in cold water

and a spoonful of vinegar. This helps improve the color and taste as well.

- **Catch fruit flies**. You may have heard the old aphorism, "You will catch more flies with honey than with vinegar." Ponder the double meaning: sure, you will get further in life if you are nice to others, but vinegar really will help you catch flies. Get the fruit flies out of the kitchen with apple cider vinegar.
    - Pour a cup or more of apple cider vinegar into a small bowl and cover the solution with plastic wrap. Next, poke the wrap with just enough holes so fruit flies can fly in, but cannot fly out.
- **Scale fish**. If you are short on time, then just rub your fish with apple cider vinegar a few minutes before scaling and you will make the process much easier and faster.
- **Meat tenderizer** (and marinade). In addition to helping you with fish, vinegar marinates beef, venison, ham or poultry as a meat tenderizer. This is the reason commercial marinades contain vinegar. You can make a marinade and save money.
    - To use vinegar as a meat tenderizing marinade, moisten it with white vinegar and rub a mixture of dry spices, herbs, and seasonings on the meat. The process not only adds flavor, but a vinegar wash will kill bacteria and simultaneously tenderize your meat or poultry.
- **Enhances nutrients in soups**. Apple cider vinegar brings out the nutrients of broth, so your soups are delicious and more nutritious. I usually use the equivalent of a few drops per bowl.

Preserves and Pickles Food

The reason you use vinegar in pickling is that the pH is highly alkaline. It is so high, that bacteria cannot grow. Vinegar will keep your produce from turning brown.

- **Keeps produce from browning**. Some people will not eat cut apples that have turned brown, but vinegar can do the trick to make this healthful snack look more appetizing. You can prevent cut apples, pears, or potatoes from darkening by placing your produce in a bowl of water with two tablespoons of white vinegar until ready to use. That is just enough vinegar to work and not affect the taste.
- **Preserve olives and pimentos**. Vinegar also helps olives and pimentos last indefinitely in your refrigerator.
- **Pickle vegetables**. Take a cucumber; add vinegar and soon you will have a pickle. Pickling is the process of preserving foods in vinegar (or another acid).

Digestive Tonic and Probiotic

Apple cider vinegar has natural sediment with pectin, trace minerals, beneficial bacteria, and is loaded probiotic enzymes – it is ideal to aid in digestion.

Vinegar is a cure-all for bloating, gas, heartburn, and indigestion, along with a host of other ailments. Vinegar promotes digestion and pH balance and supports a healthy immune system. It helps remove toxins in the body and eases urinary tract infections, helping your body to heal itself.

- **Detoxifies.** Apple cider vinegar offers powerful detoxification, which changes the pH of your digestive tract.
- **Probiotic.** It replenishes the beneficial bacteria and probiotics enzymes in the stomach.
- **Fights acid reflux.** In supporting digestion, apple cider vinegar again comes to the rescue. Try taking one or two tablespoons apple cider vinegar in eight ounces of water before you eat.

A Superfood

Apple cider vinegar adds nutritive value to your diet. It is an incredible superfood. Use apple cider vinegar for detoxification and improved digestion, as well as for a quick burst of energy.

- **Nutritious.** Apple cider vinegar is highly nutritious. It is rich in proteolytic enzymes and minerals, such as calcium (for strong bones), potassium (to help prevent brittle teeth, hair loss, and runny noses); pectin; and magnesium.
- **Energizes.** For a quick burst of energy, drink a small glass of apple cider vinegar.
- **Satiates.** Studies show vinegar increases satiety after a bread meal, which is another great reason for preppers to stock vinegar in times where food may be in short supply.
- It can also help with weight control.

Medical Conditions

As Americans mix a deadly cocktail of steroids, hormones, and antibiotics for their "health," it is nice to know that for preppers (and anyone else) there is apple cider vinegar: a natural remedy. Used both internally and externally, apple cider vinegar can support health for those with a variety of medical conditions.

- **It lowers cholesterol and supports the liver.** Vinegar with the natural sediment of pectin helps reduce cholesterol levels to lower the risk of cardiovascular disease. The reason being is that apple cider vinegar, when consumed, supports bile production to break down cholesterol.
- **It helps diabetics maintain sugar levels.** Take two teaspoons of apple cider vinegar in a glass of water daily for diabetic health. Vinegar has acetic acid, which slows the digestion of starch and lowers the rising glucose.
- **Supports weight loss, makes you feel fuller.** Apple cider vinegar has an alkaline effect on your body. The acid in apple cider vinegar increases metabolism to support weight loss, but the real benefit to preppers is that apple cider vinegar makes you feel fuller.
    - One or two tablespoons of apple cider vinegar daily for three months helps adults lose an average of three pounds.
    - You can stir it into a glass of water and drink it before meals or mix it with oil to make a salad dressing.
- **It improves heart health.** Apple cider vinegar has been medically shown to lower blood pressure.
- **Reduces night sweats associated with menopause.** Apple cider vinegar can even aid menopausal women with night sweats.

Soothes Skin

Apple cider vinegar is a natural antibacterial and helps a variety of skin conditions from eczema to aging brown spots and even warts.

- **Acne remedy.** Applied topically, apple cider vinegar has anti-inflammatory properties and kills the bacteria that thrive in acne. Best of all it will return your skin to its natural pH balance.
- **Bites and stings.** Vinegar helps soothe insect bites or jellyfish stings. Just pour apple cider vinegar directly onto the afflicted area.
- **Eczema.** Apple cider vinegar can be used to treat eczema.
- **Ringworm**. Apple cider vinegar can combat ringworm and other parasites.
- **Sunburn.** Soak a washcloth in vinegar to immediately feel the soothing benefits of vinegar.
- **Wart removal.** One component of vinegar, salicylic acid, is used on warts to remove them.
- **Wound healing.** Use apple cider vinegar for cleansing and healing wounds. Vinegar can kill bacterial pathogens. Vinegar has acetic acid, which is a powerful antiseptic.

Minor Ailments

Use apple cider vinegar as a tonic to relieve dozens of everyday ailments.

- **Yeast infection.** Soak a cloth with apple cider vinegar and apply it to an external itchy yeast prone area. The vinegar will sting momentarily and then begin to heal and soothe the itchiness. Continue application until the infection is gone. Also, drink pure cranberry juice.

- **Soothes dry throats and coughs.** Mix honey and vinegar to soothe coughs. Gargle with vinegar and enjoy the benefits of fermentation.
- **Relieves aching muscles.** Vinegar relieves muscle pain from exercise or heavy work. Pour about a cup of apple cider vinegar into a bathtub.

Cosmetic

While vinegar is helpful to clean your bathroom, you will find another reason to stock vinegar in your powder room. Vinegar offers an economical way to keep you looking beautiful.

- **Facial toner**. Apple cider vinegar can be used as a facial toner and has a cosmetic value to get rid of age spots. Apple cider vinegar can provide a natural peel to reduce the unwanted brown spots associated with aging.
- **Haircare (dandruff)**. A regimen for dandruff treatment is to combine vinegar with water before shampooing to naturally slough off dandruff.
- **Mouthwash** that whitens teeth. Gargle with vinegar. Apple cider vinegar is a natural antibacterial. As a mouthwash, you will clean dentures or whiten your teeth.

Cleans, Deodorizes, and Disinfects

Apple cider is an ideal non-toxic disinfectant that also cleans and deodorizes.

- **Birdbath**. A birdbath attracts a variety of birds, which helps to keep the insect population down. Change the water every other day and once a month wash out the birdbath with vinegar.
- **Clean water bottles**. A mixture of baking soda and vinegar in hot water will keep your re-usable water bottles fresh and clean, particularly bottles that have a narrow mouth.
- **Grass stains**. White vinegar can help you get fresher laundry by diluting one cup of white vinegar with two cups of water to get rid of grass stains. It can also help you get bolder whites.
- **Skunk**. It can help you get the stink out if you have been skunked.
- **Stains**. You can make a paste to apply directly to the stain mixing vinegar with borax to oxidize the stains away. Vinegar removes the lime deposit inside your tea kettle. Just boil a bit of vinegar with the water.
- **Clean copper or brass**. Dip a cloth in vinegar, then in salt and you can remove the tarnish off old brass or copper.
- **Dirty window**. Apple cider vinegar helps you clean the sludge from windows. Mix with water and you will make a window squeaky clean.
- **Icy windshield**. If you dislike scraping ice off your windshield, you can ice-proof your car windows with a solution of 2/3 vinegar and 1/3 water. Pour the mixture into a spray bottle and spray on windows to melt away the ice.

Homestead

Around the homestead, you will find apple cider vinegar eminently useful.

- **Vinegar removes rust.** As a rust remover, apple cider vinegar (or even white vinegar), with lemon juice, is very effective.
- **Helps around the chicken coop.** Research the many uses of vinegar around the chicken coop.
- **Stops lye from burning skin**. If you make lye soap, be sure to have a little spray bottle of vinegar handy to spray on your skin to soothe it should you get lye on your body. Wear gloves and goggles but pour vinegar in a small spray bottle as a precaution.
- **Kills weeds.** As an herbicide, twenty percent vinegar is a staple in organic gardening. Twenty-percent acidity vinegar is not for human consumption or to be used in pickling.

Germs, Viruses, Bacteria, and Mold

The science is murky on whether vinegar kills all germs, viruses, mold, and bacteria. Kill is a strong word, and the jury is still out, but it seems to help.

- **Does apple cider vinegar kill germs?** Apple cider vinegar is an exceptional product in the kitchen or the bathroom, particularly when it comes to killing germs; however, vinegar is not a disinfectant recognized by the FDA, and there is no scientific evidence that it kills dangerous bacteria like staphylococcus.
- **Does apple cider vinegar kill viruses?** The jury is still out on whether apple cider vinegar is an antiviral (effective against viruses). Certainly, vinegar is a natural antibiotic. Though antibiotics do not affect viruses, apple cider vinegar seems to be helpful.

- **Does apple cider vinegar kill bacteria?** Yes. Vinegar is an agent that kills or inhibits the growth of a microorganism when applied topically or taken orally. Vinegar is ideal for pickling because the pH is so high that no bacteria can grow.
- **Vinegar** can help prevent bacterial food poisoning. Wash your fruit and veggies with some apple cider vinegar.

Makes Stuff Last Longer

Vinegar will be extremely useful in a "make do" scenario, such as an economic depression.

- **Burnishes scissors**. Vinegar can get rid of the gunk stuck to your scissors.
- **Polish silver.** To polish your silver with vinegar, soak your silver in a mixture of half a cup white vinegar and two tablespoons baking soda for a couple of hours. Then you need only to wipe away the oxidation and your silver will be bright and shiny again.
- Vinegar is a natural solvent.
- Vinegar can help you get the sticky mess from labels on jars.

Which is Best?

There are several kinds of vinegar, each with benefits for preppers. The best vinegar is raw, unfiltered, and unpasteurized apple cider vinegar such as Braggs, because it has all the enzymes and minerals useful to preppers.

Vinegar is the product of two phases of fermentation starting with a sugary liquid, such as grape juice or apple cider. In the first phase of fermentation, the yeast converts the sugar to alcohol. In the next phase of fermentation, the bacteria convert the alcohol to acetic acid.

Vinegar (fruit or grain varieties) has many benefits for preppers.

- **Apple cider vinegar (fruit).** Apple cider vinegar seems to have the most health benefits. Eat an "apple a day" with apple cider vinegar. Apple cider vinegar has been linked with reducing hot flashes in menopausal women, as an aid for diabetes, acid reflux, weight loss, and hair care, among many other uses.
- **Red wine vinegar (fruit).** Red wine vinegar contains the same important antioxidants as red wine, but without the alcohol.
- **White vinegar (grain).** Distilled white vinegar is suited to pickling and cooking. But for preppers, white vinegar is ideal for soothing skin irritations, such as sunburn, bites (bees, mosquitoes, fleas, and ticks), rashes, and more.

Does Vinegar Go Bad?

Eventually, everything expires, but you can rest assured that apple cider vinegar has a long shelf life. Generally, apple cider vinegar has an expiration date of five years. White vinegar can last much longer, upwards of ten years. It will eventually expire, but probably it will not affect you because you will use it up.

FEED A FAMILY OF FOUR

This plan is THE fastest, cheapest, and easiest way to start a food storage program. You could complete this project in a weekend. There are no hassles with rotating, just pack it and forget. It is space-efficient – everything is consolidated into a few 5-gallon buckets. You will sleep content in knowing that you have a one-year food supply on hand for your family, should you ever need it. This method should feed a family of four, one meal per day, for one year.

Except for dairy and vitamin B12, this bean soup recipe will fulfill all your basic nutritional needs. It will not fill all of your wants, but using this as your starting point, you can add other stuff you desire.

All told, the food and storing supplies listed below cost me about three-hundred dollars.

What You Need

- 8 5-gallon buckets
- 8 gamma lids[4]
- 8 large Mylar bags
- 8 - 2,000 cc oxygen absorbers[5]
- A couple of handfuls of bay leaves
- 90 lbs of Basmati rice
- 22 lbs of kidney beans
- 22 lbs of barley
- 22 lbs of yellow lentils
- 5.5 lbs of split green peas
- 5.5 lbs of garbanzo beans
- 1 lb of salt
- A large box each of beef and chicken bouillon
- A measuring cup

What to Do

Install the gamma lids on the bucket and insert the Mylar bags. Place half a dozen bay leaves at the bottom of each of the Mylar bags and fill the bags (as instructed below), adding more bay leaves after each is one-third full until the bags are filled. Add the bay leaves after the second third and when filled. Place an oxygen absorber at the top. Label the buckets with the contents and date.

---

[4] A gamma lid is a two-part lid. The first part attaches to the bucket and the second part screws into the first part. This enables an easy to operate lid that opens and closes on the bucket.

[5] An oxygen absorber is a small packet that removes oxygen from a container. It prevents the buildup of bacteria because there is no oxygen for it to feed.

Fill

1. Fill three buckets with rice (shake it down well. Get it all in there.)
2. Fill one bucket (lined with a Mylar bag) with kidney beans
3. Fill one bucket (lined with a Mylar bag) with barley
4. Fill one bucket (lined with a Mylar bag) with yellow lentils
5. Put the split green peas in a Mylar bag
6. Put the garbanzo beans in a Mylar bag
7. In one bucket, store the split green peas, garbanzo beans, salt, measuring cup, and bouillon. (I removed the bouillon from the box and vacuum sealed it as bouillon contains a small amount of oil.)

Yes, that is a total of seven buckets, so far.

I placed a broom handle across the bucket and wrapped the ends of the Mylar bag over the broom handle to give me some support. Then slowly and smoothly I ran a hot iron over the Mylar bag to seal all except the last two inches. Then I pressed out as much air as possible before sealing the remaining two inches.

Make sure your Mylar is completely sealed from end to end. Now, stuff the bag into the bucket and rotate the gamma lid into place. This will protect your food for about twenty-five years. You will have excess Mylar bag at the top. Do not cut it off. If you have to open the containers to access the contents, you will have enough of the bag remaining to reseal.

Where to Store It

It is relatively easy to find a place for seven to eight 5-gallon buckets even in the smallest of apartments. Line the back of a large closet with the buckets. I made a couch-table by stacking buckets two high between the couch and the wall. The buckets are about six inches taller than the back of the couch. Add a shelf and drape and it looks fine; it makes a convenient place for a lamp and books. Get creative.

Recipe

Measure out:

- 8 oz. of rice
- 2 oz. of red kidney beans
- 2 oz. of pearl barley
- 2 oz. of lentils
- 1 oz. of split green peas
- 1 oz. of chickpeas/garbanzo's

Add six to seven quarts of water. Add bouillon or salt to taste. Then add any other meats, vegetables, potatoes, and seasonings (garlic) you have on hand. Bring to a boil and then let simmer for two hours. You should have enough to feed four people for two days. This is thick and hearty. You will be warm on the inside and full, with one large bowl per person per day.

When the Emergency is Over

This system allows you to open the Mylar bags, retrieve as much of the ingredients as is needed and then reseal everything after the emergency has passed. Just be sure to replace the ingredients used so that you always have a one-year supply.

The Eighth Bucket

The contents of this bucket are not included in the $300. This falls into the "what I want" category. As money and resources became available, I would just go crazy adding all of my indulgences, starting with coffee. You can add what you want, but I would fill it with dried onion. Bean soup without onion is not bean soup. Sprinkle on the onions just before serving. Hemp seeds, bacon bits, wakame, soup nuts: whatever suits your taste Beef jerky adds protein and zest to the bean soup

Practice

Buy small bags of the ingredients and fix a big pot of bean soup for dinner. Eat the leftovers the second night, and third night, until it is all gone. Find out now – rather than later – what your family might like to add. Anything tastes great the first time but quickly becomes boring after the third or fourth repeat. Do not wait until the emergency happens to discover what you SHOULD have stored in your eighth bucket.

CANNING

Canning is one of the best ways to preserve your food for the long term. Canning can be just simple items (jams) to full meals (stir fry). When you mention canning to the average person, they may think of their grandmother's canning jams or sauces.

That is just one aspect of canning and I will share with you different types and what they are used for. You must use caution since if canning is done incorrectly it can lead to food poisoning, botulism, or worse.

Some preppers choose to seal foods with the help of oxygen absorbers; others seal jars by baking the contents in an oven to create a pressure seal; still, others use a vacuum sealer or pressure canner. The most common and popular method is using a pressure cooker.

Pressure Canning

For most methods mentioned below, I have suggested the tools and equipment that you will need.

- 3-piece canning jars – includes jar, flat lid, and ring
- Canning specific pressure pot
- A rack that will fit into the bottom of your canning pot.
    - This will lift the jars away from the direct heat of the burner and allow water to circulate more easily, decreasing the chance of breakage.
- Jar lifter[6]
- Magnetic lid lift (optional)
- Tongs
- Wide mouth funnel
- A few clean kitchen towels
- Heat-safe measuring cup
- Soup ladle

Before you start, you will need to purchase a pressure canning pot.

Pressure canning can be dangerous if you do not follow your manufacturer's instructions carefully; pressure cookers and canners can explode if not used properly.

The following method is used for low-acid foods:

1. Before you start, make sure your hands and all the tools you will be using are clean.

---

[6] A scissor like device that is used to lift a hot jar out of boiling water.

2. Remove the lids and rings from your canning jars. If you are re-using jars, be sure that you are not using any with cracks or chips. Keep in mind that canning lids can only be used once, so do not reuse old ones – buy fresh lids before you begin.
3. Place the canning lids and rings into a small saucepan. Cover with water and bring to a low simmer for a few minutes. This will soften the sealing strips around the edges of the lids.
4. Meanwhile, using a wide mouth funnel, carefully fill the jars with your product. Depending on what you will be canning, you will need to leave about half an inch of space at the top of the jar.
5. With tongs or a magnetic lid lifter, remove the lids from the simmering water and place them onto the jars and seal with the circular bands using just your fingertips so that they are secure, but not too tight.
6. Wipe any spills or excess product from the lid and sides of your jars using a damp cloth.
7. Before you start canning, be sure your pressure canner has been thoroughly cleaned. Also check that the sealing ring, the overpressure plug on the cover, and the compression gasket are not cracked or deformed.
8. Prepare your pressure canner pot lid based on the manufacturer's instructions.
9. Place the canning rack into the bottom of your pressure canner along with three quarts of hot water (the amount of water may vary based on the size of your canner – refer to the manufacturer's instructions for the specific amount).
10. Place your filled jars with secured lids on top of the canning rack. You must always use a canning rack to keep the jars away from the

direct heat of the burner, which can lead to breaking or cracking.

11. Place the lid on the pressure canner and secure it tightly.
12. Heat the pressure canner over medium-high until a steady flow of steam can be seen or heard coming from the vent. Allow the steam to flow from the vent for the time called for in your recipe.
13. When the timer goes off, turn off the heat and leave the canner to cool. DO NOT open the canner.
14. Allow the pressure to drop on its own; this will take some time.
15. When the pressure has completely reduced and the air vent/cover lock has dropped, then you are ready to open the canner.
16. Remove the cover of your pressure canner. With a jar lifter, remove the jars from the pot.
17. Allow your jars to cool.
18. Remove the round outer bands from your lids and test your seals by lifting the jar by the flat lid a few inches from the countertop. The jar should lift without any separation. Jars with good seals can be kept in a cool dark place for many years.
19. A broken seal does not mean that your product has gone bad, it just has a shorter shelf life. Those jars should be placed directly into the refrigerator and used within two weeks or until the product has spoilage, whichever occurs first.

Boiling Water Canning

For high-acid foods:

CANNING

1. Before you start, make sure your hands and all of the tools you will be using are clean.
2. Remove the lids and rings from your jars. If you are re-using jars that you have had around the house, be sure that you are not using any with cracks or chips. Keep in mind that canning lids can only be used once.
3. Place a round rack into the bottom of your canning pot, then place your canning jars on top of the rack.
4. Fill the pot, and jars, with enough water to cover them. Bring to a boil.
5. Place the lids into a small saucepan. Cover with water and bring to a low simmer. This will soften the sealing strip around the edge of the lid.
6. While your jars and lids are sterilizing, prepare the product that you will be canning. When your recipe is complete, carefully remove the jars from the water using a jar lifter. Pour the water from the jars back into the canning pot. Set the jars on a clean towel. Keep the canning pot water at a simmer; you will need to boil the jars again once they have been filled.
7. Using a wide-mouth funnel, carefully fill the jars with your product. Depending on what you will be canning, you will need to leave about half an inch of space at the top of the jar.
8. Clean the rims of the jars with a damp paper towel or clean kitchen towel.
9. With tongs or a magnetic lid lifter, remove the lids from the simmering water and place them on a clean towel.
10. Place the lids with warm seals directly onto the jars and seal with the round bands using just your fingertips so that they are secure, but not too tight.
11. Carefully lower the jars back into your canning pot of boiling water using the jar lifter. Remove

any water as needed with a heat-safe measuring cup to prevent overflow.

12. Start your timer once the water has returned to a boil. Cook time will vary depending on your recipe.
13. As soon as the timer goes off, quickly and carefully remove the jars using the jar lifter. Place them on the clean towels to cool. You should hear a "ping" sound shortly after you remove the jars from the water. This means that the seal has formed. You will also notice that the lid becomes concave once the seal has taken hold.
14. Allow your jars to cool for twenty-four hours. Remove the round outer bands from your lids and test your seals by lifting the jar by the flat lid a few inches from the countertop. The jar should lift without any separation.
15. A broken seal does not mean that your product has gone bad, it just has a shorter shelf life. Those jars should be placed directly into the refrigerator and used within two weeks or until the product has spoilage, whichever occurs first.

Dry Pack Canning

Dry pack canning is selecting dry foods to store for the long term in sterilized mason jars, (as opposed to wet-pack canning as with jams, salsas, soups, and the like mentioned above). You can store pasta, cereals, corn, and rice, or pack meals such as pancake and biscuit mixes or complete dinners in a jar.

Vacuum-sealed food in the form of dry pack canning is a necessary component of your preparedness plans. One of the best tools to help you is a Food Saver. The Food Saver jar seal accessory will help you can dry foods and create vacuum-sealed protection.

Oxygen Absorber Dry Canning

The easiest method of dry canning is with oxygen absorbers. The active ingredient in oxygen absorbers is a chemical compound, powdered iron oxide. While they are not edible, they are not toxic. No harmful gases are created, and the removal of the oxygen does not affect the fresh smell or taste of the food. Dry goods paired in a jar with oxygen absorbers makes for an easy way to start canning. Dry canning in jars does not require heat to seal the lid. The job of sealing the lid takes place with the help of oxygen absorbers.

To get started, you will need oxygen absorbers, canning jars with rings and lids, and food to dry can. For example, you may like to dry can Cheerios cereal if you have small children. Start with clean canning jars (boil them and dry them thoroughly). Put your dry food and the oxygen absorber inside the can and seal. The absorber does the job of sealing the can properly. You will hear a pop when the absorber has sealed the lid.

- **NOTE**: Prepper web sites may advise you to use hand warmers instead of oxygen absorbers, but DO NOT use hand warmers with food. Using hand warmers with food is misguided advice because they are not food-safe. Instead, use them to keep your hands and feet warm. Use oxygen absorbers for your food.

For larger quantities of dried goods, choose food-grade buckets paired with Mylar (and an oxygen absorber). Food grade buckets are lined with a special plastic that is free from toxins that would absorb into your food. In this method, you will place your food into

Mylar bags with the appropriate oxygen absorbers, then seal the Mylar bags and store them in your food grade bucket. The oxygen absorber has two purposes: first, it removes the oxygen so little critters do not live in your food reserve, and second, your food stays fresh.

Food Saver Dry Canning

Another easy way to dry can is to secure your contents in a mason jar with all the air sucked out. In short, it is vacuum sealing. You can vacuum-seal food quickly and easily with a Food Saver and a special attachment to your wide-mouth mason jars. You do not need an oxygen absorber with a Food Saver vacuum seal.

Keep in mind, this is not a way to preserve food that would normally turn and spoil. This is just used to protect food from getting stale and infested with bugs.

Oven Canning

A little trickier is dry-pack canning with heat, also called oven canning. Dry pack canning is a good way to get new preppers to start canning, though it is not without a bit of warning.

1. Prepare jars for canning. Handle your mason jars with care for dry pack canning the same way you would for your other canning projects. Run them through the dishwasher to clean and sanitize them.
2. Preheat oven to 200 degrees and place a cookie sheet inside.
3. When your canning jars are dry and ready, fill them with dried goods, such as pasta or

cereals. Be sure to leave the lids off for this step.

NOTE: Do not choose foods with moisture content, such as raisins, which will do fine in jars but would be dried out with heat treatment.

4. When the oven has reached 200 degrees, remove the cookie sheet and place the filled jars on the sheet and bake for an hour.
5. Work quickly to remove your cookie sheet from the oven and place it on a good working surface. With a damp paper towel, wipe the mouth of the jars and place lids firmly on the jars. For added measure, you can throw in an oxygen absorber or a bay leaf (to keep the bugs at bay). When you hear a popping sound, your jars are sealed.

If you have a few jars that do not pop, do not worry too much. You can mark them for first use on your rotation system. At least they will be bug-free.

NOTE: Do not try this with foods that will melt under heat, such as candies or chocolate.

WARNING: Using the oven canning method can be dangerous if done improperly. The danger is the glass can explode in your oven. If not done correctly bacteria might be allowed to flourish.

6. The finishing touch is to put the filled jars in a cool oven, then set the jars at 225 degrees for 30 minutes per quart to dry can them. This method will help extend your supply by up to five years.

List of Foods to Dry Pack Can

- Beans and Legumes
- Banana Chips - Do Not Apply Heat Method
- Baking Soda
- Baking Powder
- Biscuit Mix
- Breadcrumbs
- Cake Mixes
- Cheddar Cheese Powder
- Candy (Bubblegum, Jellybeans, Hard Candies) – Do Not Use Heat Method
- Cereals
- Crackers
- Corn
- Cornmeal
- Couscous
- Dried Soup Mixes
- Wheat
- Lentils
- Oats
- Pancake Mixes
- Pasta
- Pretzels
- Potato Flakes
- Powdered Milk
- Raisins
- Rice (White rice varieties, not brown rice which has too much oil)
- Sugar (Brown Sugar: do not use an oxygen absorber and do not use the heat method.)
- Sour Cream Powder
- Sunflower Seeds
- Seasoning Mixes (ranch dressing powders, taco seasonings, soup mix)

Note: Things like nuts and chocolate chips, can also be dry canned, but they have a very short shelf life. Chocolate chips will start to turn in color.

Foods to Can

- Sloppy Joe's
- Chicken Broccoli Stir Fry
- Vegetable Stir Fry
- Tomato Sauce (You do make your own, right?)
- Jams (You do make your own, right?)
- Scalloped Potatoes
- Mac and Cheese
- Soups
- Chili
- Vegetable Stir-Fry
- Sauces
- Salsa
- Beef and Broccoli

Canning Equipment List

1. Canning funnel to help you get the goodies inside your mason jar.
2. Canning tongs to help you lift the cans from the hot water.
3. Lid lifter
4. Jar lifter
5. Jar opener to help you more easily release the pressure seal.
6. Mason jars (do not use cheap brands)
7. Jar lids (never reuse these, they nick easily, and a small nick makes the jar unusable because the seal will not be tight enough). You can reuse the bands.

8. Jar-sealer for Food Saver
9. Pressure cooker pot. Do NOT use an Insta-pot; it is not designed for the pressure needed to do canning.

Always check the seals on your Mason jars before opening them. Whenever I do an inventory, which is about once a month, I also check the seals on all my Mason jars at that time.

When I finish canning a batch of anything, I label with masking tape and ALWAYS put a date on it. I then put those items behind the older products. Remember, First In, First Out.

You can purchase stock can rotators in many places or build your own.

PLANTS

Experience has shown that when the SHTF, fresh produce becomes scarce and prices will rise. For this reason, you, as a prepper, must learn how to garden and forage for edible wild plants.

You will want to start stocking up on seeds for your garden and learn how to harvest and preserve seeds for future needs.

Another option that goes hand in hand with gardening is something I highly recommend. I cover aquaponics gardening in another book, Doomsday Bunker Book. This is the use of a large container of water that houses edible fish, specifically tilapia. Above is a bed of plants. The water circulates from the fish tank to the plants and then back down. The waste from the fish supplies nutrients to the plants which in turn cleans the water for the fish.

That is an oversimplification of the process, but read my Doomsday Bunker Book and do some research.

We all know vegetables and fruits that you buy in the store are safe to eat, but what about alternative wild edibles?

Below are a few common (North American) goodies that are safe to eat if you find yourself stuck in the wild. Please note that you need to be certain about what you are collecting as survival food. If you are not sure – leave it alone.

Here are just a few edible plants. You can confirm what they look like through a simple Google search.

Acorns

Acorns are highly recognizable, but they tend to be bitter. They should be eaten in limited quantities after being roasted.

Asparagus

This vegetable grows in the wild in most of Europe and parts of North Africa, West Asia, and North America. Wild asparagus has a much thinner stalk than the grocery-store variety. It is a great source of vitamin C, thiamine, potassium, and vitamin B6. Eat it raw, fry it, or boil it as you would at home.

Beach Lovage

Use the leaves raw in salads or salsas, or cooked in soups, with rice, or in mixed cooked greens. Beach lovage can have a strong flavor and is best used as a seasoning, like parsley, rather than eaten on its own. Beach lovage tastes best before its flowers appear. It is also called Scotch lovage, sea lovage, and wild celery.

Black Locust Flowers

Black Locust is native to the Appalachian Mountain area and is considered an invasive species elsewhere. It grows quickly, often in clusters, crowding out native vegetation. The roots alter the nitrogen content of the soil. Most parts of the tree are toxic, causing digestive system problems. Only the flowers are edible.

Blackberries

Many wild berries are not safe to eat. That said, wild blackberries are 100% safe and are easily recognizable. They have red branches with long thorns similar to a rose, the green leaves are wide and jagged. They are best to find in the spring. Their white flowers bloom, clustered all around the bush with five-point flowers. The berries ripen around August to September.

Blueberries

Blueberries grow wild in many places and are delicious when ripe. The flowers are said to be edible as well.

Cattail

Known as cattails or punks in North America, and bullrush and reedmace in England, this plant is usually found near the edges of freshwater wetlands. The best part of the stem is near the bottom where the plant is mainly white. Either boil (as you would spinach) or eat the stem raw.

Chickweed

Chickweed usually appears between May and July. You can eat the leaves, high in vitamins and minerals, raw or boiled. Pregnant and breast-feeding women should consult a physician before use.

Dandelions

Easily recognized, the dandelions in the spring show their bright yellow buds. You can eat them in their entirety raw or cook them to remove the bitterness. In spring they are usually less bitter. Dandelions are packed with vitamins A, C, and beta carotene.

Daylily

You can find this plant in many parts of the country. These are not Tigerlily or easterlies (which are toxic); a daylily is completely safe to eat. Daylilies have bright orange flowers that come straight out of the ground, with a primary leafless stem. This feature allows you to confirm it is a daylily. You can eat them whole, cook them or put them in salads.

Elderberries

An elderberry shrub can grow to a height of ten feet. The leaf structure is usually seven main leaves on a long stretched out stem, the leaves are long and round and have jagged edges. These plants are most easy to identify in the spring as they blossom white clustered flowers that resemble an umbrella. Mark the spot and harvest the berries when they are ripe, around September.

Elderberries are known for their flu and cold healing properties; you can make jelly with them. They are sweet and delicious.

Fiddleheads

The term "fiddleheads" refers to the unfurling young sprouts of ferns. They are edible only in their early growth phase, first thing in the spring.

Garlic Grass

Garlic grass is an herbal treat found often in fields, pastures, and forests. It resembles cultivated garlic or spring onions, with thinner shoots. Use it in sandwiches, salads, pesto or chopped on main courses as you would scallions.

Garlic Mustard

This plant has multiple edible parts: flowers, leaves, roots, and seeds. Leaves can be eaten year-round; when the weather gets hot, the leaves will have a bitter taste. Flowers can be chopped and tossed into salads. The roots are best collected in early spring and late fall when no flower stalks are present. Garlic mustard roots taste somewhat like horseradish.

Goose Tongue

Use the young leaves raw in salads, or cooked in soups, in mixed cooked greens, or in any dish that calls for cooking greens. Goose tongue is best in spring and early summer before the flowers appear. Goose tongue can be confused with poisonous arrowgrass, so careful identification is essential. Goose tongue is also called seashore plantain.

Gooseberries

These are common in the woods in northern Missouri, the branches are gray with long red thorns, and leaves that are bright green with five points. The leaves have rounded edges and look similar to maple leaves. The berries ripen late May through early June.

Hazelnuts

Hazelnut trees are short and are around twelve to twenty feet tall with bright green leaves with pointed edges. The nuts grow in long strands of pods and generally ripen by September and October.

Herb Robert

The entire plant is edible. Fresh leaves can be used in salads or to make tea. The flower, leaves, and root can be dried and stored for later use as a tea or as herbs as a nutrient booster. Rubbing fresh leaves on the skin is known to repel mosquitoes, and the entire plant fends off rabbits and deer, protecting your garden. (As with all herbs, pregnant and breastfeeding women should consult a physician first before use.)

Hickory Nuts

Hickory nut trees can grow to a height of about fifty to sixty feet. Their pointed-edged green leaves are spear like and can grow very large, and the nuts are round. They tend to ripen in September or October.

Jerusalem Artichoke

Jerusalem Artichokes have delicious small tubers on the roots. It is a native plant, with a very misleading name. It is not at all related to artichokes, nor does it grow in Jerusalem.

Kudzu

The entirety of this invasive plant is edible and known for its medicinal value. The leaves can be eaten raw, steamed, or boiled. The root can be eaten as well. (Like all herbs, pregnant women and breast-feeding woman should consult a physician first before use)

Lamb's Quarters

Use the raw leaves in salads, or cooked in soups, in mixed cooked greens, or in any dish that calls for cooking greens. Lamb's Quarters are susceptible to leaf miner insects; be careful to harvest plants that are not infested. Although lamb's quarters are best harvested before the flowers appear, the fresh young tips can be collected all summer. Lamb's quarters is also called pigweed, fat hen, and goosefoot.

Mallow

Mallow is a soft tasty leaf that is good in fresh salads. Use it like lettuce and other leafy greens. Toss in salads or cook it as you would other tender greens like spinach. The larger leaves can be used for stuffing, like grape leaves. The seed pods are also edible while green.

Mayapple

This plant has large deeply cut leaves with a single large white flower under its leaves. One of the first plants to come up in the spring, it is found in the forest, with the yellow fruit covered by their leaves.

CAUTION: Do not eat the fruit until it is ripe. Ripe fruits are yellow and soft. Unripe fruits are greenish and not soft.

Milk Thistle

Milk thistle is known for its medicinal use in preventing and repairing liver damage. However, most parts of the plant are also edible and tasty. Leaves can be de-spined for use as salad greens or sautéed like collard greens; water-soaked stems prepared like asparagus; roots boiled or baked; flower pods used like artichoke heads.

Miner's Lettuce

The leaves can be eaten raw or cooked. Although it has a fairly bland flavor with a mucilaginous texture, miner's lettuce works well in a salad. The young leaves are best, older leaves can turn bitter especially in the summer, particularly if the plant is growing in a hot dry location. Individual leaves are fairly small, but produced in abundance and easily picked. Stalks, bulbs, and flowers can be eaten raw. The boiled and peeled root is very small and labor-intensive to harvest and has the flavor of chestnuts.

Mint

Mint or Mentha belongs to the Lamiaceae family, which contains approximately fifteen to twenty plant species, including peppermint, spearmint, and my favorite, chocolate mint. It is a popular herb that can be used fresh or dried in many dishes and infusions. Mint oil is a common ingredient of toothpaste, gum, candy, and beauty products.

Monkeyflower

Use the leaves raw in salads, or cooked in soups, mixed cooked greens, or any dish that calls for cooking greens. Monkeyflower is best before the flowers appear, although the flowers are also edible and are good in salads or as a garnish.

Mulberries

Mulberry leaves are of two types: spade shape, and a five-fingered leaf. Both have pointed edges. The health benefits of mulberries include their ability to improve digestion, lower cholesterol, and blood pressure. It can aid in weight loss, increased circulation, and boost the immune system. Mulberries may also have anti-cancer benefits.

Common Mullein

Edible parts: Leaves and flowers. The flowers are fragrant and taste sweet, the leaves are not fragrant and taste slightly bitter. This plant is best known for a good cup of tea. Containing vitamins B2, B5, B12, and D, choline, hesperidin, para-aminobenzoic acid, magnesium, and sulfur, mullein tea is primarily valued as an effective treatment for coughs and lung disorders.

Mushrooms

Mushrooms grow everywhere, but you have to know how to differentiate between edible and poisonous mushrooms. If you are not sure, stay away.

Pecans

The trees mature at a height of around twenty to thirty feet; some can grow to one-hundred feet tall. The leaves are bright green and long with smooth edges, and the pecans themselves are in green pods. When ripe, the pods open and the seeds fall to the ground.

Pigweed

The whole plant is edible. The Amaranth seed is small and very nutritious and easy to harvest, the seed grain is used to make flour for baking. Roasting the seeds can enhance the flavor, you can sprout the raw seeds using them in salads, and sandwiches, etc. Young leaves can be eaten raw or cooked like spinach, sautéed, etc. Fresh or dried pigweed leaves can be used to make tea.

Pine

There are over a hundred different species of pine. The food can be used as nourishment as well as medicinal purposes. Simmer a bowl of water and add some pine needles to make tea. Native Americans used to ground up pine to cure scurvy; it is rich in vitamin C.

Pineapple Weed

Edible parts: pineapple weed flowers and leaves are a tasty finger food. The flowers can be dried out and crushed to be used as flour. Pineapple weed is good as a tea. Native Americans used a leaf infusion (medicine prepared by steeping flower or leaves in a liquid without boiling) for gas pains and as a laxative.

Plantain

This is another plant that thrives on the edge of gardens and driveways. Pick the edible green, rippled leaves and leave the tall flower stems. Blanch the leaves and sauté with some butter and garlic just as you would with kale or any other tough green.

Prickly Pear Cactus

Found in the deserts of North America, the prickly pear cactus is a very tasty and nutritional plant that can help you survive if you are stranded in a desert. The fruit of the prickly pear cactus resembles a red or purplish pear, hence the name. Before eating the plant, carefully remove the small spines on the outer skin, or else it will feel like you are swallowing a porcupine. You can also eat the young stem of the prickly pear cactus. It is best to boil the stems before eating.

Purslane

Although considered an obnoxious weed in the United States, purslane can provide much-needed vitamins and minerals in a wilderness survival situation. It is a small plant with smooth fat leaves that have a refreshingly sour taste. Purslane's growing season begins in the summer and extends to the start of fall. You can eat purslane raw or boiled. To remove the sour taste, boil the leaves before eating.

Self-Heal Herb

Edible parts: the young leaves and stems can be eaten raw in salads; the whole plant can be boiled and eaten as a potherb, and the aerial parts of the plant can be powdered and brewed in a cold infusion to make a tasty beverage. The plant contains vitamins A, C, and K, as well as flavonoids. The plant can, in its entirety, be used as a poultice. A mouthwash made from an infusion of the whole plant can be used to treat sore throats, thrush, and gum infections. A tea made from the plant can be used to treat diarrhea and internal bleeding. (Like all herbs, pregnant women and breastfeeding women should consult a physician first before use.)

Sheep Sorrel

Although native to Europe and Asia, sheep sorrel has taken root in North America. It is a common weed in fields, grasslands, and woodlands. Sheep sorrel has a tall, reddish stem and can reach heights of eighteen inches. It contains oxalates and should not be eaten in large quantities. You can eat the leaves raw. They have a nice tart, almost lemony flavor.

Sweet Rocket

This plant is often mistaken for Phlox. Phlox has five petals, Sweet Rocket has just four. The flowers are deep lavender, and sometimes pink to white. The plant is part of the mustard family, which also includes radishes, broccoli, cabbage, cauliflower, and, mustard. The plant and flowers are edible but bitter. The flowers can be added to green salads. The young leaves can also be added to your salad greens. The seed can also be sprouted and added to salads. NOTE: It is not the same variety as the herb commonly called Rocket, which is used as a green in salads.

Trout Lily

Also known as dogtooth violet, and adder's tongue; these bright yellow flowers are the first to bloom in the spring, with small pointy leaves. They are found in the forest and can be eaten raw.

Violets

Violets are cultivated in France for perfume. This is an incredible edible. The leaves are high in vitamin C and A. I use both the leaves and flowers in salads. Keep in mind that late-season plants without flowers may be confused with inedible greens. Forage this plant only when it is in bloom.

Walnuts

Walnut trees are the tallest nut tree in North America; they range from thirty to 130 feet tall. The leaf structure is very similar to the pecan. Leaves are spear like and grow on a long stem with six to eight on each side. The leaves' edges are smooth and green. The walnuts tend to grow in clusters and ripen in the fall.

Water Cress

Cresses (garden cress, water cress, rock cress, and pepper cress) are leafy greens long cultivated in much of Northern Europe. They have a spicy tang and are great in salads, sandwiches, and soups.

Wild Bee Balm

Edible parts: Leaves boiled for tea, used for seasoning, chewed raw or dried; flowers edible. Wild bee balm tastes like oregano and mint. The taste of bee balm is reminiscent of citrus with soft mingling of lemon and orange. The red flowers have a minty flavor. Any place you use oregano, you can use bee balm blossoms. The leaves and flower petals can also be used in both fruit and regular salads. The leaves have a similar taste to Earl Gray Tea and can be used as a substitute.

Wild Black Cherry

Wild black cherries are edible but do not eat them raw. Only use the cherries that are still on the branches and are deep black, not red. Do not eat cherries you find on the ground: cyanide, a poison, develops in them.

Wild Grape Vine

Edible parts: Grapes and leaves. The ripe grape can be eaten but tastes better after the first frost. Juicing the grapes or making wine is the most common use of this fruit. The leaves can be blanched and frozen for use throughout the winter months.

If you cut them open, the vines can supply a good source of fresh and pure water.

Wild Leeks

Wild Leeks are onion-like plants that grow in the deep woods. They come up in the spring, with edible leaves and bulbs. This plant can be mistaken for others potentially resulting in ill effects. Wild leeks can be identified by smell. If the plant does not smell like onions, they are not wild leeks.

Wild Mustard

Wild mustard blooms during February and March. You can eat all parts of the plant – seeds, flowers, and leaves.

Wild Onions

Wild onions and wild chives grow in fields. Plant chives in your yard and it will come up faithfully year after year. The whole plant may be chopped into salads, soups, chili, and stews. Likewise, for wild garlic, if you are lucky enough to find this elusive plant. There is some evidence that eating wild onions, wild garlic or wild chives may reduce blood pressure and lower blood sugar.

Wood Sorrel

You will find wood sorrel everywhere. The flowers can range from white to bright yellow and its greenery is clover shaped. Humans have used wood sorrel for food and medicine for millennia. The leaves are a great source of vitamin C. Wood sorrel roots can be boiled and they are starchy and taste a bit like a potato.

Yellow Rocket

This plant grows in damp places such as hedges, stream banks, and waysides, and flowers between May and August. The yellow rocket was cultivated in England as an early salad vegetable. It makes a wonderful salad green when young and the greens are also an excellent vegetable if treated kindly. Lightly steam or gently sweat in butter until just wilted. The unopened inflorescences can also be picked and steamed like broccoli.

PAIN REMEDIES

Pain – the biochemical signal that tells us something in our body has been damaged – is an unwelcome visitor. For those who experience pain every day due to arthritis, migraines, tendonitis, or other chronic conditions, it may be tempting to turn to chemical pain-relievers to find relief. Before doing so, open the door of Mother Nature's medicine cabinet and take a look at her list of natural pain-relievers.

I am not promising a cure or remedy for anything, just some things to consider.

Aloe Juice

We all know that aloe vera gel is at the top of the list for treating burns. What most do not know is that aloe juice is also an excellent remedy for stomach ulcers. Ulcers are painful lesions in the lining of the stomach which cause nausea, weakness from blood loss, and extreme pain. Drinking aloe juice twice daily not only helps to relieve these symptoms, but it has also been shown to speed healing of this painful condition.

Dark Cherries

According to a study performed at the John Hopkins Pain Treatment Center, anthocyanins – a group of bioflavonoids or plant pigments found in cherries and other dark fruits are effective in blocking pain signals caused by inflammation. Enjoy a serving of twenty cherries to alleviate joint aches, gastrointestinal discomfort, PMS symptoms, and other pain caused by inflammation.

Ginger Root

Ginger root is another aspirin-mimicking anti-inflammatory. A daily supplement of powdered ginger has been shown to lessen aches and pains from physical exertion through suppression of the body's production of toxic compounds known to cause inflammation and tissue damage. A ginger paste may be similarly effective when applied topically to sore joints and muscles.

Chewing on a slice of fresh ginger root is also effective for treating stomach pain and nausea, as well as for preventing morning sickness.

Cold-Water Fish

Among the many health benefits of adding cold-water fish like herring, mackerel, tuna, salmon, and sardines to your diet are the impacts on chronic pain from back and neck injuries and assistance in alleviating the pain from damaged joints. Additionally, Omega-3 fatty acids in cold-water fish improve cardiovascular function and decrease inflammation of damaged cartilage, promoting healing and overall good health.

Papaya
The enzyme papain found in the flesh of papaya fruit is a natural anti-inflammatory that works well in conjunction with bromelain (found in pineapple juice and stems) to reduce pain and swelling. Papaya extract may be taken as a supplement: the fruit is full of antioxidants and vitamins.

Tahini
Made from ground sesame seeds, tahini is a delicious dish that delivers a high dose of magnesium, a mineral most people are deficient in.

Turmeric
Curcumin, a natural phenol present in turmeric root, is another natural anti-inflammatory. Add this fragrant golden spice to your list of pain-fighting foods for a boost of flavor and beautiful color. I often add turmeric to eggs and other dishes to add a bit of color on top of its health benefits.

Hot Peppers
Capsaicin, the chemical that makes hot peppers hot is a common ingredient in many topical pain relievers. Capsaicin overloads nerves, draining them of substance-P – one of the chemical messengers that carries pain signals to the brain. Hot pepper extract offers a fast effective pain remedy (albeit temporary) pain remedy. Buy capsaicin cream at any drug store or make your own. Wear protective gloves and eyewear when handling hot peppers.

Peppermint
Peppermint can assist with muscle spasms. For sore hands and feet, apply peppermint oil to wrists and

ankles. To ease a bad headache, rub crushed peppermint leaves on your temples or brew some peppermint tea for a muscle-relaxing treat.

Yogurt

Human intestines are home to billions of microflora which are necessary for digestive health. When these symbiotic organisms become unbalanced (called dysbiosis), we may experience any number of health problems, many of which often seem unrelated to the gut (painful rashes, hair loss, hormone imbalance, etc.) Yogurt containing live and active cultures might help to repopulate and stabilize these microbes assist with such conditions as IBS, excessive gas, and painful bloating.

NATURAL REMEDIES

In this book, there are many suggestions in addressing health. These statements have not been evaluated by the Food and Drug Administration. Nothing herein is intended to diagnose, treat, cure, or prevent any disease.

Here I share with you some powerful plant remedies that have been used for ages.

Medicinal Herbs

Many plants can be used as natural remedies. Here are a few of the more potent medicinal ones that you can find in the wild that might help with minor injuries, scrapes, bites, and pains. These include:

Cayenne pepper

- Boosts metabolism

- Appetite control

Chamomile

This plant has antimicrobial properties and can be used to treat minor infections. Other common ailments that can be alleviated by chamomile are:

- Upset stomach
- Stomach cramps
- Stomach flu
- Insomnia
- Stress
- Menstrual cramps

Cinnamon

- Sugar control
- Lower blood pressure

Echinacea

Echinacea can help boost your immune system and help you fight off the flu, colds, bronchitis, and other infections.

Garlic

- Lower blood pressure
- Lower cholesterol
- Boost immunity
- Helps prevent colds
- Wards off vampires (sorry, I had to throw that in)

Ginger

- Treat nausea
- Arthritis
- Reduce inflammation

Gingko

Gingko may improve memory and circulation.

Ginseng

Taking a ginseng supplement or some ginseng tea to help with and to boost immunity against the flu.

A cup of ginseng tea can also help.

Leek

Consumption can reduce blood pressure. This vegetable also contains:

- Calcium for bone health
- Iron
- Folate acid
- Niacin
- Thiamin

Oregano

Oregano is an antioxidant and contains:

- Vitamin K
- Vitamin E
- Calcium, iron, manganese

Peppermint

- Nausea
- Improve mood
- Relieves irritable bowel syndrome
- Improve focus

Rosemary

- Improve brain function
- Improve mood
- Promote hair growth

St. John's Wort

Mostly used for its antidepressant qualities, St. John's Wort can also be used for insomnia and to help heal some wounds.

Turmeric

- Reduce inflammation
- Antioxidant
- Arthritis
- Diabetes

Simple Plant Remedies

To keep your family healthy through difficult times, learn about simple plant remedies. You will be surprised how beneficial many herbs and plants can be to you.

Avoid

Primary alert: avoid any plant with three leaves. Remember the motto, "Leaves of three, leave them be." Most often, these are poison ivy, oak, or sumac.

Contact with urushiol, the compound of the plants that irritates the skin, can lead to the following symptoms.

- Redness
- Itching
- Swelling
- Blisters

Jewelweed

If you have had the unfortunate experience of "engaging" with one of the plants mentioned above, you will be happy to know that, odds are jewelweed is nearby. Most often, this source of solace grows near to your nemeses.

Jewelweed presents a bright orange flower; the parts that grow above the ground can be medicinal. Take jewelweed by mouth to treat mild digestive disorders, and rashes caused by poison ivy. You can rub jewelweed leaves directly on the skin to relieve the pain and itch of poison ivy.

Stinging Nettle

Stinging nettles can indeed "sting" but they can also alleviate the pain caused by:

- Allergies
- Anemia
- Arthritis
- Bronchitis
- Burns

- Fatigue
- Internal bleeding
- Kidney stones
- Parasites
- Poor circulation
- Urinary tract infections

Dandelion

Dandelion, although classified as a weed, is also an herbal remedy that can help treat infections and liver problems. It is also a powerful diuretic.

ELECTRICITY

In many doomsday scenarios, public utilities will probably be inoperative or discontinued. There have been many weather events where electricity has been out for weeks at a time. An EMP, nuclear attack, or CME can all wipe out power for several weeks, or months.

In this chapter, I will address the subject of electricity.

Before any bad weather appears on the horizon, I make sure all my batteries are charged.

Food

You probably have a pantry filled with food, cans and jars, and more. It is likely you also have a refrigerator and freezer stocked full of food.

I also keep freezer packs that will help keep the freezer cold for longer, should the electricity go out.

Some people keep bottles of frozen water in their freezers to retain cold. A side benefit of this approach is that you have more stored water.

When the electricity goes out, first eat your refrigerated, then your frozen food before eating any of the other food in your pantry. You want to eat your food FIFO: First in first out, prioritizing consumption of that which will spoil first.

Batteries

You likely have all kinds of devices that can or do work on battery power. For example, radios, lights, flashlights, laptops, tablets, and cell phones.

Make sure you have a good stock of all the batteries you will need for all of your devices.

A great option is a battery bank to power and charge your devices. More on that under solar.

Marine (boat) batteries, when connected to low-watt devices, can run for hours before being fully depleted.

Solar

The options for solar power are evolving swiftly. I share a few pointers that might assist you. Those current as of this writing might not apply as you read this as technology is evolving.

Assembling a solar system is far from an inexpensive or easy endeavor. Keep in mind this project is for the long term.

You will want to have as much battery storage as possible and have room for expansion. Batteries are not cheap, and the technology evolves constantly. Build your system with that in mind.

Generator

There are many options available: choose wisely. There are battery, gas-powered, propane-powered, and inverter generators. There are also dual-fuel generators that can use either gasoline or propane.

It is best is to get a generator with as much power (KWH) as possible enabling you to run as many devices as possible. KWH is "kilowatt-hour" and a measure of power. Purchase much as you can afford to energize as many devices as possible.

Safety first: keep your generator at least twenty feet away from your house.

Make sure you have enough fuel to operate your generator for at least a month. You do not want to operate it 24/7, as that would quickly use up your fuel and wear out the machine. However, you should run it for a few hours and then turn it off for a few hours.

Inverter Generators

Inverter generators normally cost more than portable generators of comparable output but are much quieter than their conventional counterparts.

They run more efficiently and produce fewer emissions than portable generators.

Tips

Below are some tips to make getting by with less electricity more feasible. You will want to make whatever battery power you have last as long as possible.

- You should consider running your basic appliances on a schedule to save as much fuel as possible.

- Insulate your shelter for heat and cooling to reduce power consumption.
- To help save fuel, have a plan for staying warm without electrical heat and staying cool without air conditioning. This means you will have more emergency power.
- Moving to a sunrise to sunset schedule will be a necessity to conserve power for lighting.
- Store foods through dry preservation rather than refrigeration.
- Use low-amp basic appliances
- You also do not want to attract attention to yourself: generators make a significant amount of noise.
- Unplug devices when not in use from inverters, generators, etc. as each can slowly drain power (called "phantom" power loss), even when certain devices are "off".

Summary

Have as many options as possible. You can have both a solar and a generator system. Make sure your battery bank is as large as you can afford. Always keep it charged.

We are all used to our creature comforts and having electricity will help make your life easier in the event of TEOTWAWKI.

FIRE

Fire is one of the most important things you will need in any situation. You will require it for lighting, heating, cooking, drinking, and more. A fire has many other benefits, including keeping mosquitoes away and deterring other pests from entering your campsite; it also provides a cozy atmosphere.

When building a fire, remember that a fire needs fuel, heat, and air to burn. Once a fire is started, it creates its own heat.

Fire building is an art with many forms of expression. It only takes one match to start a fire, but there are many ways to build one. You can build the classic, "Teepee fire" or the "A-frame" fire. One of the key steps for building a successful campfire is determination.

Depending on weather conditions and what is available, it might be more difficult to start a fire than you think. Below are some ideas to get you going.

Learning how to build a campfire is a critical survival skill.

Building Techniques

To build a campfire you will need to gather tinder, kindling, and firewood, have a firestarter handy, and create a safe place to build your fire. You will also need a way to extinguish the fire safely.

Tinder

Tinder is the light and fluffy material that can ignite and catch a flame easily. It helps you start fires, but it is not a fire starter. Tinder ignites with minimal heat and effort. Tinder should burn the instant a lighted match touches it. Good tinder in nature snaps as you break it and does not crumble or bend. Tinder can include twigs, tops of dried weeds, and wood shavings, bark, straw, and dead grasses; there are also other man-made options, such as dryer lint.

Kindling

Kindling is a bundle of the littles sticks you will gather that can be as thin as a pencil or as thick as a thumb. Kindling should snap, and not crumble or bend.

Firewood

Firewood consists of large sticks and logs. In fire building, the fuel is the larger wood that keeps your fire going. Wood should be seasoned (cut wood that was dried for at least six months). The larger the wood, the longer your fire will burn.

Firestarter

There are many kinds of fire starters ranging from a simple match or lighter to flintstones. A fire starter can also be a magnifying glass, a Fresnel lens, or friction. Preppers generally carry with them two kinds of firestarters, such as a BIC lighter and some matches. Below are some examples of fire starters.

- BIC lighter
- Zippo lighter
- Fresnel Lens
- Ferro rod
- Magnifying glass
- I have also heard that matches can be used to start fires

Accelerant

An accelerant is any substance that will aid the spread of fire; you may not need one. An accelerant can give you the edge for survival and success in fire-building. There are many kinds of accelerants you can purchase or find among the materials you already have in your home.

- Gasoline
- Alcohol
- Lighter fluid
- Neosporin is a fire accelerant because it is a petroleum-based product.
- Vaseline petroleum jelly is an accelerant.
- Vicks VapoRub is another petroleum-based accelerant
- Wax

Safe Place

Be sure to set up your fire on sand, rocks, or dirt (never at the base of a tree or near other flammable material). Safety also includes tying your hair and ensuring no sweatshirt draw-strings or scarves are dangling. Have tongs and a mitt ready, too.

Extinguishing the Fire

Before you start a fire, you should have a bucket of water on hand. Never start something you cannot stop, and water is your first defense at a campfire. Experienced campers know that you do not need to dump the whole bucket to extinguish your flames. You need to stir the embers while pouring water to completely put out the fire and use your hand to make sure there is no warmth. Never leave a lit fire unattended.

Types of Fire

Get started on your fire-building skills by learning and practicing some of the different methods discussed below.

Teepee

A classic way to build a fire is the Boy Scout method, which is to make a teepee design. It is perhaps the most well-loved method of fire starting because it makes an efficient fire, it lights easily, and it is also relatively easy to build and maintain.

A-Frame

To build a fire the Girl Scout way, you will make an A-frame rack with several pieces of kindling, then put the tinder on this rack (instead of on the ground). The tinder has air underneath it and space for you to light the fire with a match or other fire starter.

Log cabin

The log cabin fire requires the same basic materials of tinder, kindling, and fuel (logs). A log cabin fire lights easily and grows efficiently – once you build it you will not have to do much maintenance. You will not have to continue adding wood to it, so you can truly enjoy your fire.

Self-Feeding

Want a fire that lasts all night long? An experienced fire builder will appreciate the self-feeding fire that can last fourteen or more hours. The self-feeding fire is a clever contraption.

Make a "V" by hammering large branches into the ground with about a foot between the base where they are in the ground. Then lay two large logs side by side on the ground. Add other logs along the "V" going up the sides.

Start your fire on top of the bottom-most logs. When they burn, other logs will slowly roll into the fire adding more fuel. The fire will burn for many hours.

The Hand-Drill

The hand-drill method is the most primitive, the most primal, and the most difficult to do. All you need is wood, tireless hands, and some determination. Here is how it is done:

Build a tinder nest that will be used to create the flame you get from the spark you are about to create. Make the tinder nest out of anything that catches fire easily, like dry grass, leaves, and bark.

Cut a "V"-shaped notch into your fire board and make a small depression adjacent to it.

Place bark underneath the notch. The bark will be used to catch an ember from the friction between the spindle[7] and fireboard.

Place the spindle into the depression on your fireboard. Your spindle should be about two feet long for this to work properly. Maintain pressure on the board and start rolling the spindle between your hands, running them quickly down the spindle. Keep doing this until an ember is formed on the fireboard.

---

[7] The spindle is the vertical stick that you roll between your hands.

Once you see a glowing ember, tap the fire board to drop your ember onto the piece of bark. Quickly transfer the bark to your nest of tinder. Gently blow on it to start your flame.

Fire plow

Prepare your fireboard by cutting a groove in it for the track of the spindle. Take the tip of your spindle and place it in the groove of your fireboard. Start rubbing the tip of the spindle up and down the groove.

Have your tinder nest at the end of the fireboard, so that you will plow embers into it as you are rubbing. Once you catch one, blow the nest gently to get the fire going.

Bow Drill

The bow drill is probably the most effective friction-based method to use because it is easier to maintain the speed and pressure you need to create enough friction to start a fire. In addition to the spindle and fireboard, you will also need a socket and a bow.

Make a socket that is used to put pressure on the top end of the spindle as you are rotating it with the bow. The socket can be a stone or another piece of wood. If you use another piece of wood, try to find a piece that is harder than that which you are using for the spindle. Wood with sap and oil are good as it creates a lubricant between the spindle and the socket.

The bow should be about as long as your arm. Use a flexible piece of wood that has a slight curve. The string of the bow can be anything. A shoelace, rope, or a strong vine. Just find something that will not break. String up your bow and you are ready to go.

Cut a V-shaped notch and create a depression adjacent to it in the fireboard. Underneath the notch, place your tinder.

Catch the spindle in a loop of the bowstring. Place one end of the spindle in the fireboard and apply pressure on the other end with your socket.

Using your bow, start sawing back and forth. You have created a rudimentary mechanical drill. The spindle should be rotating quickly. Keep sawing until you create an ember.

Drop the ember into the tinder nest and blow on it gently. You will need patience as it can take some time.

Flint and Steel

It is a good idea to carry around a good flint and steel set with you at all times. Matches can get wet and be become useless, but you can still get a spark from putting steel to a good piece of flint.

If you are caught without a flint and steel set, you can always improvise by using quartzite and the steel blade of your pocketknife. You will also need a char cloth (see below for instructions on how to make a char cloth). Char cloth catches a spark and keeps it smoldering without bursting into flames. If you do not have char cloth, a piece of fungus or birch will do.

Hold a piece of rock between your thumb and forefinger. Make sure an edge is hanging out a couple of inches. Grasp the char cloth between your thumb and the flint.

Grasp the steel striker or use the back of your knife blade. Strike the steel against the flint several times. Sparks from the steel will fly off and land on the char cloth, causing a glow.

Fold your char cloth into the tinder nest and gently blow on it to start a flame.

Char Cloth

Char cloth is created by combusting an organic material in a way that releases its gasses without burning it up completely. It can be used in conjunction with any method we discussed in this chapter.

The resulting substance has a low ignition temperature – just a single spark or point of heat can start it burning.

Once the char cloth has been set off, it will ignite your tinder more easily than had you applied the original spark/heat source directly to it. Char cloth smolders longer than a match, making it advantageous in getting slightly damp tinder going, and while matches can fail on a windy day, a sturdy breeze can help get a spark-ignited piece of char cloth going.

Char cloth can thus be a lifesaver in survival situations and makes an excellent addition to one's camping supplies or bug out bag.

Needed

You will need the following:

- **Sealable tin can.** An empty, clean shoe polish can, Altoids tin, metal Band-Aid can, etc. To make a larger batch of char cloth, you can use a coffee can, sealed with foil on the top.
- **100% cotton material.** An old t-shirt, pair of jeans, handkerchief, canvas, etc. Fabrics that contain artificial fibers will not result in a combustible material. Other organic materials like burlap also can work.
- Scissors
- Nail

How to make it

1. To ensure complete, uniform charring, cut your cotton material into strips or pieces that can be placed into your can without being rolled or folded up.

2. Make a small hole in the top of your can with a nail or other tool. The hole will allow the smoke/gasses out of the can. You do not want the hole to be too big, as this will let oxygen into the can, causing the cloth to burn.
3. Seal the container and place it on a small fire or a bed of coals. Smoke should escape from the hole in the can. If flames appear around it, that is okay.
4. Watch the can, and once it has stopped smoking, turn it over. It will begin to smoke again.
5. Once this smoke has stopped, remove the can from the fire.
6. Inspect your char cloth. It should have turned black but not become ash and feel semi-rigid without being brittle.

Lens-Based Methods

Using a lens to start a fire is an easy matchless method that many have played with. As a child, if you have used a magnifying glass to focus the sun to start a fire, then you already know what I am talking about.

To use this method, that is all you have to do. Use the magnifying glass to focus the rays of the sun to a point on your tinder and shortly you will have a flame.

Traditional Lenses

To create a fire, all you need is some sort of lens to focus sunlight on a specific spot. A magnifying glass, eyeglasses, neck of a bottle of water, or binocular lenses all work. If you add some water to the lens, you can intensify the beam. Angle the lens towards the sun to focus the beam into as small an area as possible. Put your tinder nest under this spot and you will soon have yourself a fire.

The only drawback to the lens-based method is that it only works when you have sun. So if it is nighttime or overcast, you will not have any luck.

In addition to the typical lens method, there are three odd, but effective, lens-based methods to start a fire as well.

From Ice

You can make fire from a piece of ice. All you need to do is form the ice into a lens shape and then use it as you would when starting a fire with any other lens. This method can be particularly handy for wintertime camping.

For this to work, the ice must be clear. If it is cloudy or has other impurities, it is not going to work. The best way to get a clear ice block is to fill up a bowl, cup, or a container made of foil with clear lake or pond water or melted snow. Let it freeze until it forms ice. Your block should be about two inches thick for this to work.

Use your knife to shape the ice into a lens. Remember a lens shape is thicker in the middle and narrower near the edges.

After you get the rough shape of a lens, finish the shaping of it by polishing it with your hands. The heat from your hands will melt the ice enough so you get a nice smooth surface.

Angle your ice lens toward the sun just as you would any other lens. Focus the light on your tinder nest and watch as you make a fire from ice.

Coke Can and Chocolate Bar

All you need is a soda can, a bar of chocolate, and a sunny day.

Open your bar of chocolate and start rubbing it on the bottom of the soda can. The chocolate acts as a polish and will make the bottom of the can shine like a mirror. If you do not have chocolate with you, toothpaste also works.

After polishing the bottom of your can, what you have is essentially a parabolic mirror. Sunlight will reflect off the bottom of the can, forming a single focal point. It is kind of like how a mirror telescope works.

Point the bottom of the can towards the sun. You will have created a highly focused ray of light that can be aimed directly at your tinder. Place the tinder about an inch from the reflecting light's focal point. In a few seconds, you should have a flame.

Batteries and Steel Wool

Stretch out some steel wool to about six inches long and a ½-inch wide.

Hold the steel wool in one hand and a 9-volt battery in the other. Rub the side of the battery with the "contacts" on the wool. The wool will begin to glow and burn. Gently blow on it.

You can use any battery, just touch one end of the steel wool to one pole of the battery and the other end of the steel wool to the other pole. The wool will glow and burn.

Transfer the burning steel wool to your tinder nest. The wool's flame will extinguish quickly, so do not waste any time. It would be beneficial to use a piece of char cloth to transfer the flame to your tinder.

Water Sandwich

Using a rock, crush some bark into dust. Put the dust onto another piece of bark. Put water into a Ziploc bag and shape it into a sphere. Use it as a magnifying glass under the sun to focus a beam of light onto the bark dust.

Smartphone Battery

Rub the battery's terminals against some steel wool. As it catches flame, place it in your tinder. Most modern phones do not open to allow access to the battery.

If rubbing the terminals does not work, fold one piece of the steel wool and touch it to the positive and negative terminals.

SELF-DEFENSE

I was taught that the best way to protect yourself is to have situational awareness and be strong enough to walk away from trouble, when possible. You should know what is around you at all times. I am not advocating putting your head on a swivel, but you should be cognizant of who is in your area and what is going on around you.

Imagine if you were in the middle of a crowded street, enjoying your time with your family. Suddenly, you find yourself near some drunks who start a fight, and you separate from your family, get pulled into the fray. You are a prepper, and like most preppers, you are carrying a small pistol. Do you use it?

Some would say yes – it is a time to defend your family, and that is what a weapon is for. Others would hold off – bringing deadly force into a relatively small conflict is certainly a legal issue and is probably not necessary considering that these people are drunk. With that said, this is a self-defense situation. A gunshot in a crowded public space is one of the fastest ways to start a riot, potentially getting you or your family harmed, the balance point for many tends to tip toward leaving your weapon holstered.

Imagine again, you and your family return home and see the basement window broken. Alarm bells go off in your head, and you draw your weapon, instructing the kids to wait in the car. Upon entering, you can see that the dangerous infiltrator is a teenage boy who lives down the street. You have fewer than five seconds to decide what to do.

Maybe you are one to draw in these circumstances, however, I believe that these are two examples of situations where yes, a gun could be advantageous to you, but it would be better left holstered.

Of all the four major prep areas – food, water, shelter, and defense – it is the defense that is most often overlooked. I know preppers who think that all they need is a gun and some ammunition, while others stock an armory; but for most, self-defense is simply just about the weapons you choose to keep. In reality, self-defense is so much more.

Personal Defense

The first line of defense to prepare is your last line of defense – your ability to defend your person. Guns are fantastic but are not always the best solution to a conflict. The best way to start that process is to take a martial arts class regularly.

Martial arts classes are incredibly varied, and depending on where you live, you should find a broad spectrum of different styles. You could opt for a striking art like Taekwondo, Karate, or Kung Fu, or you could focus on a martial art that emphasizes grappling such as Judo. Many arts are combinations by nature (any MMA (mixed martial arts) style or Krav

Maga), and there are many schools of striking or grappling arts that borrow from outside of the strict boundaries of their chosen style to incorporate a broad range of self-defense elements.

Striking arts are probably what everyone thinks of when they imagine martial arts, as they are based on using your hands and feet to punch, chop, and kick your way to safety. These arts value speed and brainpower, over size and physical power and often incorporate a large variety of cardio exercise practices that will double as your workout for the day. The major advantage of learning a striking art is clear – these arts are focused on disabling an opponent quickly from a relative distance and allow you at least a chance of fending off multiple opponents. A typical class will involve practicing kata or patterns of movements, practicing kicks and punches against air, striking heavy bags or padded opponents, and jumping techniques.

Grappling arts are more like wrestling rather than what you would likely think of as “martial arts” techniques. Instead of punches and kicks, you will learn disabling holds, pressure points, and throws. A certain amount of size and strength is not necessarily essential but will help. Classes for grappling arts tend to emphasize a one-on-one, back-and-forth style of practice, and may not be as exercise-heavy as the striking arts. The advantages of studying a grappling art are that they focus on defending yourself against abductions and mugging-style grabs and unarmed defense against an armed opponent, which are highly practical scenarios. Many people who have studied street fights have noted that over eighty percent of these encounters end up on the ground, where grapplers have a distinct advantage.

Both styles give you opportunities to practice against your classmates in simulated fighting scenarios. Striking courses usually incorporate sparring practice where you use heavy pads and light contact to simulate a fight and test your reflexes and skills. This allows you to safely practice so that you will know you can function in times when you need to defend yourself. Grappling arts use amateur wrestling, or kneeling wrestling; you maneuver your opponent on the mat to attempt to make them submit from a painful or inescapable hold.

Finding a style is a good choice, but it may be better to find a school first and a style second. Not all martial arts courses are created equally. Many are black belt factories, where you pay a certain fee and are guaranteed a black belt after a certain amount of time. Other schools are going to emphasize tournament performance or flashy-but-not-realistic jumping and leaping attacks. Good schools are hard to come by, but they will offer a variety of different types of skills and performance elements, have a wide variety of people at varying levels of abilities and ages, and have experienced instructors. Ask for a free trial class, or at least to be allowed to watch a class before signing up.

Non-Gun Weapons

In addition to a basic level of skill in hand-to-hand combat, I think it is also important to find a hand-to-hand weapon to supplement your firearm and EDC kit. My personal choice is a tactical flashlight that functions as a striking weapon with a strobe light to distract and disorient my attackers. It is a tool that I can use in my everyday life. Some models of tactical flashlights have stun guns or preprogrammed S.O.S. signals that can add to their functionality, and since it is a small flashlight it is a very inconspicuous weapon that is never confiscated at sporting events or theme parks. If you do not like that suggestion, consider some of these other hand-to-hand weapons that are easy to carry.

- Pepper spray
- Taser
- Brass knuckles
- Stun guns
- Small hand tools like hammers, and screwdrivers
- Keys
- Nun chucks
- Hardened forearm armor
- Expanding batons
- Fixed-blade knife
- Folding pocket knife
- BB gun
- Pellet gun

Remember that regardless of which weapon(s) you choose to carry, you should be well prepared and ready to use it/them. A knife may not be the best weapon for every encounter, but if that is what you choose, that is what you might be stuck with to defend yourself. If you pull pepper spray from your pocket or purse, know how to use it, or it will be taken away and used against you.

Dogs

Another suggestion for personal defense is to get a dog.

Dogs are fantastic companion animals that are often overlooked but highly practical pieces of a prepper's armory. They require much more regular upkeep than what you are storing in your gun cabinet but are also useful for a wide variety of situations.

Dogs are not a fail-safe mechanism for security. Training and mentally stimulating your dog will certainly help in developing his senses enough to make him a versatile tool and defense mechanism as well as a companion.

Training your dog to be a more aggressive "guard dog" is certainly an option, but one that I would strongly discourage. Your dog needs to be socialized among other animals and be extremely selective about whom he attacks. An "attack dog" is not a good choice, and will likely do you more harm than good, both in terms of legal trouble and difficulty in raising and training him.

If you do not want a traditional guard dog, and if your dog is more likely to lick your home invader than attack him or warn you, then do not bother – prepper dogs are a highly effective deterrent against would-be attackers.

Choosing a large breed dog will make your home significantly less appealing to any home invaders or burglars. More intelligent breeds, such as German Shepherds can act as an early warning system against people approaching your home and may be able to be put to work around your home for basic tasks if you keep livestock. These kinds of dogs are also those that have a reputation of being aggressive (even though they are not), and their reputation alone can be a deterrent. Keep in mind that many of our modern breeds, even those poorly designed for defense, like bloodhounds or greyhounds, were originally bred to be hunters or highly specialized seekers, and have many practical applications in SHTF or survival situations

Taking dogs with you when you go outside for exercise or a walk is a good way for urban preppers to discourage muggers and attackers. Even rural and suburban preppers can benefit from having a dog along on walks or runs in case of twisted ankles, or other sorts of accidents.

All told, the advantages of having an animal companion are significant, specifically in terms of defense. For those with allergies, some hypoallergenic dogs are available, and depending on the breed you choose, you may find yourself unaffected by short-haired breeds.

A dog is not the highest priority on the list but can certainly be a helpful addition to a home or personal defense system.

Self Defense Options

- **Avoid**. Most Preppers try to keep a low profile. Do not brag to anyone about having guns and ammunition or about having a two-year supply of food on hand. You are the first one the locals will loot in desperate times. Avoiding the threat is best, but aversion is not always possible.
- **Hide and Disguise**. Along the same lines of keeping a low profile, preppers hide and disguise their supplies, and are prepared to hide or disguise themselves as well. Advanced preppers may build a clandestine bunker or have a bunker in plain view that is defensible. Looking like a homeless person might be a technique of camouflage in uncertain times and could be part of a prepper's bug-out strategy to escape potential threats.
- **Diffuse**. While in America, you have the right to bear arms, you also have the right to bear hugs. Talking is the first line of a peaceable defense. Preppers may be able to engage the attacker in a dialog to diffuse the fight. The big secret to winning a fight is to never get hit in the first place.
- **Surprise**. The element of surprise is also a defense tactic.
- **Gloves**. Get a supply of leather slap gloves. These gloves may look harmless, but they can

be used as a powerful blunt force defense weapon.

- **Shoes**. Consider steel-toed shoes.
- **Key Chain**. A self-defense key chain can be a person's best friend.
- **Retreat**. In some situations, retreating may be the most viable option for survival. Preppers always assess their situation and have a plan of retreat. Look for exits, plan on escapes even while you are in the middle of a struggle.
- **Revise, rethink**. Constantly rethink your situation and revise it as necessary.

Simple Ideas in Self-Defense

The best self-defense is mentally preparing for the positive outcome of an attack. If you can, create a win-win option to avoid a struggle altogether.

In the event of a confrontation, preppers have a basic knowledge of self-defense tactics to employ, including martial arts, gun safety, and marksmanship, even archery. And then there is always mace or pepper spray, a stun gun or a taser. These things all create confidence, and yet there are more effective means to self-defense to consider.

Do Not Wear a Ponytail

Having a ponytail gives an assailant something to grab. This is among the first things an attacker will look for. Wear a hat instead as that can fall off and you can escape.

Know-How to Use Your Self-Defense Weapons

Hopefully, you will have a good stash of weapons of a wide variety. Make sure you are familiar with every one of your self-defense tools and how to use them, including how to assemble, disassemble, and repair them. Practice often with all your tools and make them part of you.

When Confronted Toss the Goods

If you find yourself in a situation where an assailant wants something from you, like a purse, a wallet, or your bugout bag do not just hand it to them. Take the item and toss it in another direction and then run. From that point, you can either continue to run away or take out your gun and handle the situation. Your goal is to increase the distance between you and the other person to gain the upper hand.

Engage a Conversation

There is a psychological point where someone is assessing the situation to determine whether or not to attack you. If you ask a question, you put the other person the task of answering your question. Engaging is distracting them, and you can make your move.

Do Not Tarry

Sometimes an attacker will scope out potential victims in a shopping mall parking lot. The assailant will prey upon those who sit idle in the car, doors unlocked, checking their cell phones. Remedy the situation with the “lock and leave” approach. Lock doors promptly, then buckle up and leave. You can pull over and check e-mail once you get out of the parking lot.

Situational Awareness

Always be aware of what is going on around you and know who is near you. Always be alert to your surroundings and cognizant of an escape route. Know where the exits are, especially emergency exits or routes.

At home, have an alarm system that has a video so you can see who is around or coming to your door. These will alert you via cell phone or tablet even if you are not home.

Get to know your neighbors and who belongs and does not belong in the area. I know every regular delivery driver and utility worker by name.

If you live in a planned community, know how to get out of the area by vehicle and on foot.

Riots

Less than six months after the outbreak of Covid-19 in the United States, there was rioting. This is not the place to delve into the reasons for the riots, mayhem, destruction, looting, etc. This book is not meant to be a political forum and I will not take one side or the other.

This book is to help you prepare for such an eventuality. It essentially provides advice for most eventualities, but there are a few specific ideas that I would like to share with you in case you have to live through riots.

There are two schools of thought about what to do in the event of riots and each one has advantages and disadvantages.

SELF-DEFENSE

Bugout

The safest course of action would be to GOOD (Get Out Of Dodge). You have been practicing packing up and leaving as quickly as possible, yes? Great.

Board up your place, all windows and doors, turn off all utilities and go to your bugout location. Ideally, you would put up boards on the inside and outside of your windows and doors.

Outside, to protect your windows from being broken in. Inside to give more of a deterrent in case someone does take out the external boards. Even better would be steel plates that you can weld to the outside of your windows and doors.

The advantage of bugging out is that you are not in a position to be attacked. And, no one is the wiser to your location nor can they steal your stock of supplies and food.

The disadvantage is that your house will be vulnerable to being looted and destroyed. It is not always in the financial reach of people to have a secondary location that is fully stocked and ready for occupancy.

If you do not have a secondary location, if you have the skills and knowledge, you can bugout to the wild.

Bug-in

Although not necessarily as safe, if you have no secondary location, staying where you are is probably going to be your only option.

Hopefully, you are having your mail delivered through a slot directly into your home. Another option that would give you more privacy would be to use a mailbox service.

Some things that you can do to fortify your primary location are the same things mentioned in the above section. You should also barricade your doors from the inside. If you have a fence around your property, that would be helpful. If you have a way to electrify that fence, it will help keep predators at bay.

In advance, make sure you have yourself and your family well stocked with everything you will need. Make your house look like no one is there.

- Do not use lights at night
- Use your generator sparingly (if at all)
- Tell no one you are there
- Do not invite anyone to come over.
- Stop any subscriptions (newspapers and magazines)
- Close your curtains

Do Not Act Like a Victim

It may seem odd, but if you find yourself in a captive situation, you can gain favor first by using your name and bonding with the individual. Introducing yourself makes you an acquaintance and no longer a stranger. It is much easier to hurt a stranger and more difficult to hurt "Jennifer" or "Brad." You can gain valuable time in creating such hesitation and this may benefit your negotiations. To bond with the individual, you can be sympathetic. For example, "I'm sorry that you're short on cash, but this isn't going to solve your problem in the long run," or "I know you're hurting inside, but we can get help for you."

Conversely, if you play the role of victim, then you are making the job much easier for your assailant. When you say, "Do not hurt me," the person does not hear the "do not" they only focus on the other part of the sentence and they begin to act accordingly. When you are sympathetic, you are doing something unexpected and filling a need the person may have. You are refocusing their actions and that helps you.

Do Not Be a Girl Scout

Have you ever fully considered the Girl Scout motto which is, “To help others at all times”? This is an idea that was not carefully thought through by the Girl Scouts. It is not safe to “help others at all times” especially when you are alone. Even more so in our current times. Beware that if someone is limping, struggling with bags, or is wearing a sling or bandage, it could be part of a ploy or ruse to lure in sympathetic individuals.

DUCT TAPE

Preppers have a penchant for creative problem solving and thinking outside of the box. Some preppers do not even know there is a box. Duct tape is a favorite survival tool to get out of sticky situations. Armed with duct tape, WD-40, and a multi-tool, a prepper can fix just about anything and survive to tell the story. Unleash your inner MacGyver and start thinking about the myriad ways to use duct tape in a survival situation.

In a pinch, duct tape will repair just about anything or help you solve almost any survival problem. Whether you are mending a broken fishing pole, patching up a tent, or fixing torn clothing, duct tape might be vital for your survival. The only limit is your creativity.

Best of all, duct tape is often reusable. Reusing things is another prepper favorite, so be sure to repurpose, reuse, and recycle your duct tape.

Below are some of my favorite ways to use duct tape. I have left off some of the more common uses of duct tape which many people already know.

Avoid Being Tracked

If you are trying to evade someone who is tracking you, then you can duct tape the bottom of your shoes to cover and minimize the treads on your shoes. Tracking dogs will still be able to catch your scent, and your foot will make an imprint from your weight, but you will make it more difficult for those searching for you.

Avoid Snow Blindness

The blinding glare of snow can damage your eyes and leave you not only lost in the wilderness but permanently scarred unless you use adequate eye protection. If you did not pack any sunglasses, you can improvise by creating a superhero mask over your eyes by taping two pieces of duct tape together (sticky sides together) and cutting horizontal slits in the duct tape about an inch long enabling just enough light to pass through to allow you to see.

The telltale signs of snow blindness include a feeling of having grit in the eyes worsening with every eye movement. There is also an increased pain in the light, reddening, and often a headache. The condition heals in a few days, but risks damage to the retina, including painful photokeratitis, or macular degeneration. You can avoid these and persevere with duct tape.

Blackout Windows

In combination with a tarp or garbage bags, duct tape can help you black out your windows to help evade detection. If you are the only one in the neighborhood with light during a cataclysmic event, this will draw unwanted attention.

Similarly, you can blackout your flashlight if you need a smidgen of light but want to evade detection.

Bond Surfaces

The tight weave of duct tape contributes to its strength, making it an ideal substance to adhere strongly to a wide variety of surfaces like cloth, vinyl, leather, plastic, metal, and laminates. As well, the surface is resistant to moisture, which will help you endure weather and temperature extremes, and wherever you need a flexible and weather-proof bond. It tears easily by hand without curling and conforms to uneven surfaces. It is good for general maintenance, wrapping, sealing, and protecting.

- **Keep the floodwaters out.** When flood warnings come, you can shut the doors and use duct tape on both the outside and inside of the door to seal against water entering, along with your sandbags.
- **Seal storm windows.** With duct tape, you can seal the outside of storm windows during the winter as an added measure of protection.
- **Avoid carpet trips and falls.** Use duct tape to secure carpets and pads from shifting to help avoid slips, trips, and falls.
- **Temporary glasses repair.** Temporarily mend the arm of your prescription or sunglasses with duct tape to see your way out of danger.

Build a Fire

The fibers of duct tape can work to accelerate your fire starter. A piece of duct tape can provide about two minutes of burn time.

Make a fire with duct tape and char cloth: the fire starter lasts much longer.

Camouflage for Survival

Duct tape can help you camouflage yourself or your vehicle. In the event you need to hide a vehicle with foliage, you can use duct tape to help you layer branches, twigs, bark, moss, and leaves for cover. With the same general technique, you can also evade notice by affixing nature to your body like a ghillie suit.

Craft Survival Tools.

Everyone has a camping story to tell and duct tape is often part of the adventure. Here are some useful survival tools for camping and hiking.

- **Fix your hiking boots.** With duct tape and Krazy Glue, you can repair shoes while on the trail.
- **Fabricate snowshoes.** Learn how to make snowshoes from duct tape.
- **Make a bucket, bowl, or cup from duct tape.** Water collection is essential and if you have no bucket you can make one with duct tape. A bucket is also useful to collect berries, field greens, or small game.

- **Bag.** By folding the duct tape and taping it back to back, you can fashion a bag to hold and protect small items.
- **Fabricate a cup.** You can use the duct tape to make a cup for drinking.

Emergency Car Repairs

Whether you need to repair a broken fan belt to get to your next destination, or you blow a universal joint and need to repair it, duct tape could help you mend it temporarily and get you slowly to safety.

It is possible to repair a tire just enough to get you up the road to a gas station.

Again, these are extreme survival ideas and you will have to use your judgment about the safest alternative for you. Stash duct tape in your vehicle and you will be glad to keep the highway patrolman off your tail by temporarily fixing your taillight.

Emergency Cordage.

If you do not have paracord, you can make cordage from duct tape by rolling long strips lengthwise, folding in half, or taping two sections together. From the cordage, you can twine it into a heavier rope by braiding three pieces of your duct tape cordage. You can make a sling for your rifle from this cordage, and you can sling other gear as well. Here are other ways to use duct tape as emergency cordage:

- **Attach gear to your backpack.** Clips may break and gear may become loose, but you will have an instant solution if your bugout bag includes duct tape.

- **Tie food bags in the trees.** Tie food up in the trees to secure it from raccoons, bears, and other critters.
- **Tape a lantern to a tree.** Light the way with a flashlight or lantern by securing it with duct tape cordage to a tree.
- **Hang clothes out to dry.** If your clothes get soaked while camping by the river or lake, you can make just enough cordage to line-hang your clothes.
- Improvise shoelaces, belt, or a dog leash
- **Construct shelter camp furniture.** You can lash together a makeshift shelter or furniture using duct tape cordage.
- **Make a strap for your sunglasses.** Do not lose your glasses on the journey: make a leash from duct tape.

Fix Broken Equipment

- **Improvise a rifle sling.** Duct tape rolled lengthwise becomes instant cordage. If you have a broken strap you can repair it immediately in the field.
- **A coupler for your magazines.** By use of a coupler, you can attach two magazines for more efficiency and speed. If you do not have one, you can make one with duct tape. Even if you have a coupler, you may want to use duct tape to ensure they do not come apart.
- **Hide your magazines.** Secure magazines where others might not expect to find them, under desks for example, with duct tape.

Handcuffs, Gag

The day may come while in survival mode when you will need to restrain an intruder or a would-be defector of your group. Duct tape handcuffs might buy you some time to think. Get handy with duct tape and craft a "survival handcuff" if someone is acting up. Do not just think of duct tape in terms of handcuffs, you will want to tie them to something. Outdoors you can strap an individual to a tree or a pole. Indoors, you can tape them to a chair. For more security, make sure their hands are behind them.

Duct tape can also be used as a gag to keep the bad guys quiet. The movies always show duct tape over the mouth to silence victims, and this is something to remember in survival times.

Just as important, when it comes to duct tape handcuffs, every prepper should learn how to break free from them.

Hem a Pant Leg

It is not uncommon to hem a pant leg with duct tape; a cyclist prepper may find the use of this material as a leg cuff. Consider this for your get home bag or bugout bag, for a situation in which you must bicycle home or bugout out from the office.

Improvise a Grommet, Malice Clips, Etc.

If you need a grommet where one does not exist, puncture your cloth and reinforce it with duct tape on both sides. This could come in handy for turning tarps into tents or shelters. Using duct tape in this fashion can also help you improvise Malice clips®[8] or affix straps and webbing to your MOLLE[9] packs.

Improvise First Aid Needs

- **Bandage wounds with duct tape.** Yes, duct tape might hurt a little with hairy arms or legs, but it is surely better than bleeding to death if you do not have bandages handy. Place the dressing (gauze or a cotton ball) directly on the wound and seal with duct tape and you have a bandage.
- **Butterfly Bandage.** Devise a butterfly bandage from duct tape for deep cuts.
- **Improvise moleskin.** A person can prevent callouses and blistering of hands or heels with duct tape by placing duct tape at the point of friction. The duct tape essentially acts as an extra layer of skin to prevent soreness from rubbing.
- **Pull off ticks and chiggers.** Short on tweezers in your first aid kit? If you have duct tape, you have the means with which to pull out ticks and chiggers with a quick pat and a subsequent yank on the duct tape.
- **Make a splint or sling.** In a survival situation, you can craft a sling or splint with the help of duct tape. For a finger splint, use the touching finger to immobilize the injured one. Wrap a sprained or broken ankle so you can walk to your next destination.

---

[8] MALICE CLIPS® are injection molded, heavy duty, reusable connecting clips that are designed to attach modular pouches to MOLLE style equipment.

[9] See above in the chapter on Terms.

- **Restrict blood flow with a tourniquet.** Often confused with a sling or splint, a tourniquet is a device that forcefully constricts blood flow through compression to prevent profuse bleeding. It requires the use of a stick or baton and binding you can make with duct tape.
- **Remove splinters.** There is more than one way to remove a splinter and sticky tape is one of them.
- **Create an eye patch or sleep mask.** If your eye(s) needs a rest, you can use duct tape to keep the light out, allowing the eye(s) to relax. Just be sure to add some gauze around the eye, so you do not pull out an eyelash or strip your eyebrow. Perhaps you need to rest during the day but prefer to sleep in total darkness: a sleep mask can help.
- **Pull out a cactus spine.** If you get into a prickly situation with a prickly pear cactus you will need to remove a cactus spine. Pull it out with duct tape. Just affix duct tape over the affected area, gently pat, then yank it out briskly.
- **Transport injured.** To transport an injured person, you can make a field stretcher with duct tape. This can be useful for medics who must often improvise.

Improvise Tools for Defense and Hunting.

Every prepper knows that bullets will someday run out and that they must rely on other weapons. It is fairly easy to construct a duct tape weapon. Duct tape weapons help you hunt or can even save your life.

DUCT TAPE

- **Make a duct tape spear.** Use duct tape to affix a knife to a broomstick and you have a defensible and threatening space between you and an attacker. A duct tape spear could help you get dinner as well.
- **Magazine**. You can roll up a magazine and duct tape a pair of scissors to create some extra distance between you and an attacker
- **Fletching an arrow.** Use duct tape to craft the fletching portion of an arrow: that is the portion of the arrow that gives it “air”, with duct tape.
- **Help dress a duck.** Pluck feathers of duck with duct tape. Now that is the true use of “duck” tape. (Sorry)
- **Make a sheath for your knife.** As a sheath, duct tape will spare you from undue injury. Start by wrapping some cardboard around the knife, then wind duct tape around the cardboard.
- **Snare an animal.** Make animal snares from duct tape cordage.
- **Make a slingshot.** Use duct tape to defend yourself with a slingshot to scare away the bears or use it to knock out small game.
- **Cuff a pant leg.** Hunters can also cuff pant legs with duct tape to protect from the elements – either to keep out the ticks and chiggers or to prevent the cool air from rising the pants and stealing body warmth.
- **Patch a hole in your hip or rain boots.** If your hip boots should spring a leak while fishing, you can temporarily repair them with duct tape. This also works well for rain boots or snow boots allowing you to continue hunting or fishing in comfort.

Keep Clothing Clean and Dry

Use duct tape for your survival clothing using the "COLDER" method, a technique taught to United States Air Force pilots.

- **CLEAN**. Keeping clean: duct tape can lift off dirt or help you air dry clothing (use duct tape to line dry; for example, hanging from trees).
- **OVERHEAT**. Avoid overheating. Duct tape can provide shade if you make an umbrella, sun hat, or fan.
- **LOOSE**. Wear clothes loose and in layers. Use duct tape to make a pack for extra clothes if you do not have a backpack.
- **DRY**. Because duct tape is waterproof, it can help keep you dry along with providing an added layer of insulation. You could also craft a shelter or even an umbrella with duct tape.
- **EXAMINE**. Inspect clothes for defects in wear and use duct tape to hem cuffs or add layers of padding where needed.
- **REPAIR**. Replace zippers and repair tears with duct tape.

Keep Small Tools Together

Fishhooks, tiny batteries, needles, and screws can easily get lost if not otherwise secured to the sticky back of duct tape.

Make a Candle

You can improvise a candle from duct tape since it will ignite. Roll it around a stick and you have a small candle.

Make a Fly Trap

An unusual use for duct tape is to make "fly tape." Flies and mosquitoes who land on duct tape will get stuck to it.

Make A Hammock

You can use duct tape and a tarp to make a hammock to keep yourself above any critters. In tropical areas, you will want to build your shelter off ground, or you will be infested with insects (and covered in morning dew). In a pinch, you can also suspend food in the trees using duct tape to protect it from bears, etc.

Make a Hands-Free Flashlight

In the absence of a headlamp, you can strap a flashlight to your person or create a headlamp to light your way, which will keep your hands free to carry something, defend yourself, or to climb your way out of trouble.

Make a Hurricane Window Seal

Seal or strengthen windows against hurricanes with duct tape by making large "X" shapes to help contain the glass. Similarly, duct tape can fix a broken window after a storm or a break-in.

Make a Potholder

If you do not have a potholder to handle hot pots and pans, you can create a duct tape sleeve to shield the heat. Remember that duct tape burns, so you should not cook with duct tape on the handle.

Make Shoes Stronger

During the Great Depression, people would extend the life of their shoes by inserting cardboard, but today we have duct tape which provides a much stronger reinforcement.

Sometimes the best shoes for a hike are the old and worn ones. If they come apart, you can glue them back together.

Mark a Trail

Different colored duct tape can come in handy to mark your trail as you move through terrain to hunt or fish. Even ordinary black duct tape can help you write an S.O.S. to notify first responders of your presence in the area. You can make arrows or form letters of the alphabet. If you have a Sharpie, you can also write a message on gray or light-colored duct tape.

No Crows in Your Garden

The shiny side of the duct tape reflects sunlight and can help keep crows and other birds out of your garden.

Pad Knees and Elbows

Whether you need a little support at the knee for gardening, are evading someone, or getting in a sniping position, duct tape can help pad and protect your knees and elbows from rugged terrain.

Prepare for a Biological Attack

You can prepare for an impending biological attack by sealing the windows in your home using tarp and duct tape. Read on, I discuss it later in more detail.

Protect from Volcanic Ashes and Gas

Use some duct tape with a drop cloth or tarp to keep out volcanic ash and gas. Together they secure windows and doors. It will also aid you in keeping lights and your profile low. Again read on for more details.

Prevent Snake Bites

Since ninety-five percent of snake bites occur below the knees, duct tape secured around a hiking boot and up the pant leg could provide a sufficient barrier to penetration. In case of a snake bite, do not use a tourniquet or you will keep venom in one place, and the limb will swell resulting in possible loss of the appendage.

Protect Your Head

Whether you need a hat to shade you from the heat of the sun or to keep your head warm from the blast of winter, it is duct tape to the rescue. You can fashion a hat to fit your entire head or a visor to help keep the sun out of your eyes.

Provide a Watertight Seal

Technically speaking, duct tape is not waterproof, however, it is water-resistant. Duct tape will seal just about anything and for this reason, can help you patch stuff that might leak.

- **Repair tents and tarps**. A small tear in your tent could become a bigger problem if you do not tend to it right away. Use duct tape to keep out water, wind, and starlight.
- **Fix a leaky water bladder or bottle.** Water is life and in a survival situation, it is impossible to overstate the importance of water preservation. If the bladder of your water pouch bursts, duct tape can save the day. If you lose the lid, you can seal your water with a makeshift cap made of duct tape.
- **Hoses.** Temporarily patch leaky hoses with duct tape.

Repair Outdoor Equipment

Duct tape can help you make repairs on just about anything:

- **Tent repair.** Rips are not only a major inconvenience, but they could also threaten your wellbeing in severe weather. Duct tape can keep the water and cold out. Duct tape will also help you connect broken tent poles.
- **Canoe repair.** As mentioned above, duct tape fixes leaks, so suppose your only canoe has sprung a leak and you need it to get down the river. Duct tape may get you to your destination. With enough duct tape, you can craft a paddle using a forked branch, a bag, and duct tape.

- **Bike repair.** If you ever find yourself with a flat and without any patch, you can repair an inner tube. Duct tape is also handy on the cuffs of pants to keep them from getting caught in the bike chain.

Reseal Mylar Bags and Other Food Containers

Often a freeze-dried meal is enough for two to four people. If you are good with portion control or need less food and have another vessel with which to mix some of the dried contents with hot water, you can reseal the remaining dried portion for the next meal with duct tape.

Seal Ammo Boxes

Duct tape was originally developed during World War II to help seal ammo boxes. Preppers today who are concerned about long term storage may vacuum seal ammunition along with silica packages, however duct tape still works well to seal ammo boxes. The gasket can lose its seal and by using duct tape, you can help protect the contents from moisture.

Set Up a Quarantine

Include duct tape as part of your pandemic kit. With Ebola or other contagions such as avian flu or coronavirus, you will want securely sealing protective equipment. Use duct tape as a seal between touchpoints (gloves and boots) and as an emergency cover to prevent leaks should your Tyvek or chemical suit become breached. Learn to seal your protection equipment properly with the use of duct tape.

To set up a quarantine room, seal it with duct tape and plastic sheets around windows and doors.

Signal for Help

The reflective silver duct tape will not help you much to signal for help, but you can attract attention with duct tape on a beach by spelling out S.O.S. in the sand

Cover the rocks with the reflective duct tape and spell out the S.O.S. to make your location visible to a rescuer.

Soften Sharp Edges

Sharp edges can sometimes make a backpack unbearable. Duct tape can soften the edges to make equipment tolerable to carry.

Support Your Ankles

A traveler's tip is to wrap duct tape under socks to provide extra support for ankles, for example when standing in long lines. An ankle brace in conjunction with the duct tape may also offer support for painful ankles.

Waterproof Your Shoes

Endure extreme weather conditions with duct tape on your shoes. In bugout scenarios, you can use it to help make shoes water-resistant in rain or snow. This barrier will keep moisture from getting to your feet and wearing you down. It will also add insulation to help you endure the snow or cold weather extremes.

Stock Duct Tape in Five Places

1. **Your bugout bag.** Be sure to pack duct tape in your bugout bag. Wrap the tape around a sturdy water bottle. In this way, you will save the weight of the heavy cardboard tube.
2. **Your vehicle.** Duct tape is on the list of car essentials because it is handy for fixing leaky hoses and more.
3. **Your workplace**. Have duct tape handy at the office or your work as you can use it to improvise in so many situations from a hurricane or earthquake to defense or rioting.
4. **Home**. You will find duct tape immensely useful in survival times to repair a wide variety of things around your home.
5. **Bugout location**. Use duct tape for pandemic preparedness, window repair, first aid, and more.

Always have more on hand than you think you will need for a year.

Now you know some amazing ways to use duct tape. Get some duct tape now to ensure you have it when you need it. Duct tape is just one of many preps available for just a couple of dollars that could save your life.

Handy Tip

- If it moves and should not, use Superglue or duct tape.
- If it does not move and should, then use WD-40.

Duct tape can get you out of a bind and also help you bind stuff to save a life. There are endless possibilities for the use of duct tape. You need only a little imagination.

BLEACH

WARNING

Bleach is high on the list of prepper necessities because it helps reduce impurities and bacteria. Yet there are some cautions and, in some scenarios, better alternatives.

Never use bleach in an enclosed area (you need proper ventilation). Always use protective gear, including gloves and a face mask.

Bleach Is a Poison

While it may be okay for human consumption in diluted volumes, it is important to know that sodium hypochlorite can lead to poisoning. Sodium hypochlorite is an extremely dangerous and corrosive substance. It can cause extreme damage to skin and eyes that come into contact with it. For this reason alone, you should heed extreme caution before considering purifying water with it.

Because sodium hypochlorite is a poison, make sure you:

- Never use bleach in an enclosed area – you need proper ventilation. (I know I just said it, but it deserves repetition.)
- Do not mix ammonia and bleach as it produces a noxious vapor.
- Use gloves and eye protection when handling bleach.

Bleach Can Aggravate Asthma

If anyone in your home has asthma or breathing problems, you will want to steer clear of bleach, particularly because there may not be a doctor around and bleach can aggravate asthma.

A safer alternative to bleach is hydrogen peroxide for sensitive individuals.

Bleach Purifies Water, But…

Chlorinating your drinking water will oxidize the organic contaminants and produce cancer-causing trihalomethanes. In other words, bleach is carcinogenic. However, when boiling water is not an option and you have no other water purification methods available, then consider bleach. As a reminder, bleach is not intended for human consumption; however, FEMA advises emergency disinfection of water with bleach as a last resort. FEMA's "recipe" is about eight drops of bleach for each gallon of water.

Bleach Can Help Battle Cholera

Cholera is an infection in the small intestine caused by the bacterium *Vibrio cholerae*. Chlorination and boiling are often the least expensive and most effective means of halting the transmission of cholera.

Scented Bleach

Scented bleach is useless for purifying your water because of the added chemicals. Avoid bleaches that contain perfumes, dyes, and other additives. You have better alternatives.

Clean Your Dishes with Minimal Water

To wash dishes in the same method as used in restaurants, you will need a bucket for your composting to scrape off the excess food. Then you need three tubs. Fill the first tub with water to rinse food from the pots, plates, and utensils. Fill the second tub with warm soapy water to clean your dishes. Finally, fill the third tub with water and a teaspoon or tablespoon of chlorine bleach (unscented). This is the final rinse to sanitize. Finally, hang your dishes out to dry.

Bleach Expires

Check the bottle and you will see that bleach indeed has an expiration date. Bleach expires after about six months.

What to do with expired bleach? Put a big X on the bottle, so you will know it has expired. Now you will have liquid useful for flushing your sanitation. It will also help eliminate bad odors.

Swimming Pools Contain Bleach

Swimming pools contain as much as four parts per million of bleach. While this is the correct amount for pools to keep the water free of algae and bacteria, it is highly unacceptable and dangerous water to drink. Thinking of using your pool water reserves? Do NOT do it!

Using an above-ground pool as a reserve of water in preparation for a catastrophic event is an option many preppers employ. I would recommend against such an option as the pool structure has probably absorbed some of the chemicals and bleach. Avoid using pool water as a potable option.

Bleach is a Pesticide

Bleach can prevent, destroy, or repel pests, which means it is a pesticide. This is not a pretty picture if you are thinking of consuming it. Bleach has been used to kill bed bugs in situations of extreme invasion. Bed bugs must come in direct contact with bleach to kill them, which is why you use bleach to wash bedding infected with bed bugs.

An important note is that sodium hypochlorite is an "antimicrobial pesticide" however it will not deactivate *Giardia Lambia* or *Cryptosporidium.*

A Prepper Staple

- It helps prevent the spread of cholera. This often-fatal bacterial disease of the small intestines causes severe vomiting and diarrhea and comes about from infected water supplies.
- Disinfects cutting boards and more

BLEACH

- Gets rid of slippery moss and algae on bricks
- Kills weeds
- Kills insect eggs
- Pour bleach into standing water to eliminate insect larvae and other pests.
- Cleans trash cans
- Sanitizes surfaces
- Sterilizes water
- Removes odors
- Kills mold, and mildew
- Kills cold and flu viruses from countertops, cabinetry, and floors.
- Kills Ebola virus

VASELINE

Vaseline, petroleum jelly, is extremely useful in a survival situation. For starters, it is a popular fire accelerant, and also has several first aid uses. Go beyond thinking of Vaseline for your chapped lips and hands.

Originally called “wonder jelly,” this slime has many fascinating uses for preppers in first aid.

Chapstick is another handy survival tool because it contains petroleum jelly. If you do not have Vaseline, look to lip balm for many of the things that Vaseline does.

- **NEVER** use Vaseline for burns. Vaseline is grease and you should never apply grease to a burn. To manage burns, immerse skin in cold water. The National Institute for Health says “Grease should never be applied to a fresh burn”.

- Get a burn kit and learn how to use it.

As an Accelerant

One of the most basic survival uses of Vaseline petroleum jelly is as an accelerant to give your campfire a boost. Petroleum jelly fuels your fire in combination with tinder (it will not work without the tinder).

- **Cotton balls**. Scouts douse cotton balls in Vaseline and store them in Ziplock bags to light a campfire. Each ball will burn about ten minutes. The combination is a classic fire starter. You can mix Vaseline with any fluffy tinder you have in hand or your bugout bag.
- **Chips.** You can use Cheetos or Doritos chips with Vaseline to get your fire going. The chips will burn on their own, but the addition of Vaseline will provide a more robust and immediate flame.
- **Gauze**. Keep some gauze in your medical kit with petroleum jelly for medical use.
- **Dryer lint.** Another variation of this fire-starting method is collecting lint from the dryer to use as tinder. Mix lint with Vaseline and insert it into a tube of toilet paper. Light it with a match to start your fire.

As a Candle

Create a makeshift candle. Be sure to transfer the jelly into an appropriate vessel. Do **not** use the plastic jar that contains your jelly as it can catch fire.

Keeps Stuff from Sticking

Vaseline can be used as you would oil or grease.

- **Loosen a stuck ring**. Vaseline can help you slide off a ring from a swollen finger.
- **Firearm**. It can be used as an emergency lubrication for a firearm.
- **Keeps candle wax from sticking**. Sometimes candle wax gets stuck at the bottom of a candle holder. To help with this sticky situation, coat the inside portion with Vaseline.
- Keeps appliance racks in your refrigerator or oven from sticking.
- Ensures window casters slide smoothly
- Grease sliding doors and door hinges

Prevents Rust on Machinery

Vaseline has valuable applications for machinery and metal gadgets. Vaseline can keep your machinery in good working order and prevent rust and corrosion.

- Lubricate a bike chain should you not have a bike lubricant.
- It provides proper friction for skateboard and roller-skate wheels
- Grease keyholes to ensure locks and keys work smoothly and efficiently. Helps locks work better particularly in cold weather.
- Prevents batteries from corroding.

Help Get Zippers Unstuck

Petroleum jelly can lubricate zippers on tents, pillowcases, pants, and jackets to ensure they pull smoothly and you stay warm. Petroleum jelly is not only handy around the tent, but also your home.

Gets Rid of a Sticky Mess

Improvise the use of petroleum jelly to get rid of a sticky problem, such as resins on your hands.

- **Clean hands**. Clean dirty sticky hands with Vaseline.
- **Removes gum**. Petroleum jelly removes gum stuck to hair or wood.

Pest Control

You can use Vaseline for pest control.

- **Trap flies**. Make a fly trap with paper and petroleum jelly. Cut the paper strips and hang. Bugs land and cannot fly away: they tear their legs off trying to get out of the sticky problem.
- **Ants**. Keeps the ants away from your pet's food and the threshold of your house. Petroleum jelly acts as an invisible border.
- **Carpenter bees**. Filling in the paint cracks and holes is the best way to keep carpenter bees from destroying your house.

Shave Without Water

Petroleum jelly helps you shave without water. While most use petroleum jelly as an aftershave application to soothe the legs and face, if you are without water, you can use petroleum jelly to shave. After shaving simply wipe the legs or face clean with a towel.

First Aid

Petroleum jelly has many uses for first aid and beauty.

- It helps stitches heal better after surgery.
- Vaseline helps protect skin after minor cuts, scrapes, and mild burns should a topical antibiotic, such as Neosporin or Polysporin not be available or if you are allergic to either of those medicines.
- Vaseline protects the skin from chapping caused by extreme cold. To help heal chapped hands, put a generous portion on the hands, then cover with gloves or mittens to keep them moistened for twenty-minutes.
- Vaseline softens rough heels and elbows. Apply petroleum jelly to the feet and cover with socks and awake to softer feet.
- Vaseline relieves dry, itchy skin (eczema).
- Prevents diaper rash

Cosmetic Value

Vaseline will help you with cosmetics in numerous ways.

- **Lips**. Vaseline is a lip balm (use petroleum jelly as a lip balm or gloss).
- **Hangnails on fingers and toes**. Vaseline keeps hangnails at bay.
- **Facial or foot scrub**. Epsom salt mixed with petroleum jelly makes an excellent exfoliant scrub, use gently on the face, and to scrub away heel skin.
- Vaseline helps keeps your scalp moist (reducing dandruff).

- Vaseline provides hair sheen and reduces split ends.

Vaseline Alternatives

- **Coconut Oil**. Coconut oil thickens nicely and applies well to moisturize skin like Vaseline.
- **Honey**. Honey applied topically heals wounds, just like Vaseline.
- **Olive Oil**. Olive oil has lubricating properties, as does Vaseline.
- **Beeswax**. Beeswax is an excellent lip balm

BARTERING

Looking at life in America today, it may seem surprising that there is so little bartering. For centuries, bartering was key to our survival. Should we encounter an economic collapse or other catastrophe, bartering will likely return in full force.

People still barter in our days. For example, I will make you a cake if you give me a ride. I will run this errand for you if you can help me with this project. And so on. Humans are hard-wired to trade/exchange. Do you have stock investments? If so, you are bartering.

Bartering Tips

1. Set your price/product ceiling and stick with it. Go above it, you risk falling down a slippery slope to full price or more.

2. Know your product. It is difficult to set a fair price if you do not know the true value.
3. Be willing to walk away
4. Double up on bartering supplies.
5. In times of trouble, you can trade for food, water or medical needs
6. Physical items are not the only barterable items.
7. Knowledge and skills are also barterable and will have a high value
8. Items like water and rice will have a high barter value

Bartering Items

The following is a list of items that you may consider to add to your barter list. Before compiling your barter list stock up on your essential needs.

- **Gold and silver.** In an SHTF scenario, smaller coins and denominations are optimal. However, many people believe that precious metals will be worthless in the time of SHTF and feel that practical items will have a higher value.
- **Water filters/Life Straw.** Other people will need water and your filter will be worth a significant amount in an emergency.
- **Ammunition.** Guns are all good and well, but they are worthless if you do not have ammunition for them. Make sure to have these common ammo sizes: 9mm, .38, .22, and 12 gauge shotgun shells. You may also consider Tasers, pepper spray, and other defense devices.
- **Alcohol**. In the event of a disaster, there is going to be a time when a drink is exactly what you need, and you will not be alone. Consider small plastic bottles. Alcohol can be used

medicinally too; a person with a toothache would be happy to barter for a shot of whiskey.

- **Coffee and tea.** Caffeine is something many of us need every day. In an SHTF scenario, it can also help keep you alert, further ramping up its trade value.
- **Food/MREs.** Having extra food for trade is probably one of the easiest items to add to your bartering list. Simply stockpile additional resources to your survival foods and MREs (Meals Ready to Eat) collection. There is never such a thing as too much food in a survival situation.
- **Fuel.** Any sort of fuel: gas, diesel, propane, or kerosene, could be the source of light and heat. Propane, for example, is easy to store. For trade use the smaller camping tanks.
- **Clothing.** While adding clothing to your bartering stockpile, consider the essentials first; underwear and socks. Ensure universal sizing to make them more effective for bartering. Jackets and protective outerwear, such as rubber boots, ponchos, and gloves could also come in handy, depending on the disaster or situation and weather.
- **Medical kits/Band-aids.** First aid kits and band-aids are other valuable items.
- **Medicines/Pain meds.** In addition to basic first aid, many people need medication. Aspirin or Tylenol could become needed and highly valuable. Antibiotics or even a roll of antacid tablets could become an item of high value in a barter situation.
- **Portable solar panels.** People who did not prepare as well as you did for a disaster situation may be looking for alternative sources of power in a variety of SHTF scenarios. Charge top dollar.

BARTERING

- **Toilet paper.** Self-explanatory
- **Hygiene.** Think of other items for hygienic comfort. For example, feminine products, and moist towelettes.
- **Cigarettes.** People are addicted to their smokes and they would undoubtedly pay a high price in trade.
- **Batteries.** Batteries may be the only power source for essential items like flashlights. Batteries have a relatively long shelf life making them easier to stockpile.
- **Lightsticks.** Good for overall light in a confined area, especially for children.
- **Flashlights.** Light is essential should the grid be down, people will be looking for any alternate light sources.
- **AM/FM radios.** Radios are important, as they could be the only means of obtaining information in a disaster.
- **Walkie-Talkies.** Walkie-talkies are an easy way to communicate over short-range distances, especially if cell towers and connectivity are down.
- **Chocolate and sweets.** People are often in need of comfort in times and need.
- **Firestarters.** Firestarters can provide light, heat, and cooking sources.
- **Water containers.** A method of transporting water is essential.
- **Spices.** Consider multi-use spices and herbs; a stockpile of salt not only provides food with flavor but can also be used to preserve food. An herb like mint is not only sought after for flavor but has medicinal properties. Sugar can also fetch a high price from sweet tooth barterers.
- **Soap and cleaning products.** Soap can help tame the spread of infection, germs, and bacteria. Bars of soap are easy to store but

consider antibacterial options and other cleaning products.

- **Toothpaste and toothbrushes.** Dental health is a necessity; toothpaste, toothbrushes, and floss will be needed and desired items. Since toothbrushes do not last forever, they will always need to be replaced, making them a commonly needed barter item.
- **Deodorant.** No matter the situation, people do not like to be smelly. Deodorant and other fragrance items will always be an item that can be used in trade.
- **Solar showers.** In the absence of running water, one of the greatest luxuries would be a solar shower. They pack up small, making them easy to store, yet they provide comfort many people would consider worth trading for.
- **Garbage bags.** Garbage bags have multiple applications, including a shelter in a pinch. Their multi-purpose ability makes them great for barter.
- **Pet food.**
- **Heirloom seeds.** Seeds would be a valuable commodity in many scenarios, as growing your food could be a necessity in a variety of situations.
- **Duct tape.** Check out my chapter on duct tape. It is invaluable.
- **Condoms.** Needed for more than just the obvious.
- **Drink mixes.** Drink mixes are easy to store and have generally long shelf lives. Consider single packets instead of larger packaging as it will make it easier to trade.
- **Fishing gear.** When you cannot go to the store.
- **Multi-tools and pocketknives.** Multi-tools are the best for bartering because they cover a wide range of uses.

- **Screws, nuts, and bolts.** Basic supplies will be difficult to come by.
- **Gardening tools.** For barter or lending.
- **Firewood.** Another no brainer; fire is life and many of us will need firewood to keep us warm or to help us cook our food.
- **Tarps.** Tarps are great temporary covers, ground cover, and shelters, not to mention their various other uses. They will always be a popular trade item.
- **Rope and bungee cords.** A rope is an important survival tool in any SHTF scenario. Paracord is even better for your use and barter.
- **Lotion and Chapstick.** Dry conditions actually can provide painful situations, making lotion and chapstick necessary items for some people.
- **Sleeping bags and blankets.** People will always need a place to sleep, and in disaster situations, they could become quite the commodity.
- **Air mattresses and air pump.** Much like sleeping bags, but with higher trade value, air mattresses provide comfort and restful sleep, a priceless benefit in a survival situation. Make sure you have an air pump as well, but consider the power sources, you probably want to invest in one that comes with a manual option, a car power source, or at least something more than just a traditional electric plug.
- **Laundry detergent.** Keeping our clothes clean is psychologically beneficial, as well as beneficial to our health.
- **Soda.** I do not drink soda, nor do I stock it for myself, but I do have some for barter. Soda, much like coffee or tea, can provide a caffeine boost Sodas are also a luxury item, like chocolate, that will bring a higher trade value.

- **Candles.** I recommend a large stock of candles of different sizes.
- **Paper, pens, and pencils.** Writing is not only a form of communication, it is a way to record history, tell stories, play games, send messages, and draw pictures. Their worth is immeasurable.
- **Grooming supplies.** Grooming items are important. Items include hairbrushes, shavers, shaving cream, and combs. These will be highly sought after and useful for trade.
- **Baby supplies.** Baby diapers, wipes, formula, and food are more specialized. However, they would be valued by a parent looking for some creature comforts for their baby.
- **Books.** Those things called books that people used before "Google" may provide some use if the Internet and electricity are down. Books still hold a vast amount of knowledge that you cannot put a price on. Not to mention their entertainment value.

Bartering Knowledge

Your knowledge and skills are also things you can barter. Keep this in mind as you prepare for the next disaster. Learn some additional skills that you can use to help others at a time of TEOTWAWKI.

- Nursing
- Doctoring
- Surgery
- First aid
- CPR
- Self-defense (to be able to give lessons)
- Woodworking
- Auto mechanics

BARTERING

- Electronics
- Construction
- Electricity
- Veterinarian
- Cooking/baking
- Beekeeping
- Blacksmithing
- Hunting
- Butchering
- Plumbing
- Sewing
- Gardening
- Gunsmithing
- Fletching
- Music

TO DO LIST

The following list is for experienced preppers as well as the novices to help prepare in advance of a doomsday scenario.

There are hundreds of things you could be doing right now toward your prepping goals. A prepper's work is never done.

While the list of things one can do is endless, at some points in the prepper lifestyle you may feel as though nothing has been accomplished at all. For such times and for extra time on your hands, consider the ideas below when deciding how to wisely spend your time.

Here is my prepper's checklist of things to do today toward your prepping goals:

1. **Be happy and grateful.** Take a moment to be grateful for your current life of abundance. Be thankful for the toilet

paper, for a cup of coffee, chocolate, or electricity. Be grateful as you take a shower or a drink of water, or as you wash your clothes. Relish the abundances of life while unaffected by a disaster.

2. **Gunsmithing.** Learn how to take apart and repair weapons. This includes making your ammunition.
3. **Butchering.** Of course, you know that you have to learn how to hunt for food. However, once you have your catch, do you know what to do with it? You will need to learn how to skin and butcher.
4. **Buried treasure.** Find a few places that are not on your property, but on a route that you may take in an emergency and bury buckets of supplies. These buckets should contain a few MREs, a first aid kit, a knife, etc. These containers can give you sufficient supplies to help you last for an additional few days or weeks.
5. **Tools.** Learn how to use basic hand tools. Understand the basics of repairing things in your home.
6. **Plumbing.** Learn the basics of plumbing in case a pipe breaks or the toilet runs constantly.
7. **Create a food and supplies journal.** Take a pad of paper and write down exactly what your family eats for an entire week, right down to the snacks. You will be amazed at your family's list and how it can serve as a personalized guide to food storage.
8. **Check the list of Foods to Hoard**. Check your pantry against this list and stock up before they are gone from supermarket store shelves.
9. **Shop for bug-out clothing.** Although most look better in camouflage, you should **not**

wear such clothing directly after a disaster. You might compromise your safety if you live in an urban setting. Looking too much like military personnel is a signal to potential marauders that you have things to take.

10. **Learn how to garden.** In five days, you could sprout seeds in a seed sprouting tray, and add crunchy homegrown goodness to your sandwiches, pasta, or salads. Antioxidants found in sprouts help protect your body against free radicals. Try growing lentils, green peas, garbanzo, and mung beans.
11. **Potatoes**. Potatoes are much easier to grow than you might think.
12. **Mushrooms**. Grow mushrooms for a tasty addition to your soups, stews, pasta, and salads. You could also learn how to forage for edible mushrooms. However, be careful to learn from someone who truly knows how to detect non-poisonous mushrooms.
13. **Fire**. Learn to make a fire in more than one way.
    a. A BIC lighter is an excellent tool, but the day may come when it cracks or runs out fuel rendering it useless.
    b. A magnifying glass
    c. A magnesium stick
    d. A fire ribbon
    e. Waterproof matches.
14. **Do today's laundry** (just get caught up). Get all your laundry caught up. Yes, it is an everyday task, but today is the day to take care of your dirty laundry. Suppose the power grid goes down, and your laundry is stacked to the hilt. You would be wasting precious water and time laundering by hand tomorrow. Discover off-

grid laundry techniques and never wait until tomorrow what you can do today.

15. **Do laundry** (off-grid method). Get an inexpensive washboard and do your laundry the old-fashioned way. While you are at it, get some clothespins, hangers, and a wash line.
16. **Do your dishes** (enjoy the dishwasher). Know that the dishes you pile into the dishwasher today could be your last clean ones for the foreseeable future.
17. **Disposables**. Check your supply of paper plates, napkins, and disposable utensils. You will not want to waste precious water doing the dishes by hand if the power grid goes down.
18. **Basins**. Purchase some basins so you can do dishes by hand.
19. **Make doctors and dentists appointments.** Get a checkup while you can and do not delay surgeries. Keep current on prescriptions. Talk with your doctor and stock your cabinets with extra supplies. Check my First Aid List.
20. **Hold a yard sale or garage sale.** Shedding your home of non-essentials will not only create more space for you to stock your prepping essentials, but also provide funds to buy more prepping gear, hunting equipment, camping equipment, or food storage. Or sell your collection on eBay. Would you rather have a collection of freeze-dried food for your pantry or a collection of Star Wars memorabilia? eBay is the perfect venue to convert collections into supplies and food to complete your prepper's list of essentials.
21. **Go to a yard sale.** Now that you have held your garage sale to get rid of things you do

not need, head to a garage sale to find the things that you do. You will find plenty of emergency preparedness supplies, including used camping equipment, survival books, inexpensive bicycles, shelving, hand-crank tools, and more.

22. **Bicycle.** Check your bicycle and have repair tools on hand. Your bike might be the only mode of transportation should there be a power grid failure.
    a. Bike lock for every bike
    b. Bike repair kit
    c. Patches
    d. Tubes
    e. Chains
    f. Oil
    g. Bike pump
23. **Liquid foods.** Your food shelf space should contain ten percent of liquid foods. Any liquid foods you have will help you conserve your water supply. For example, you can make rice with chicken, beef, or vegetable stock.
24. **Water.** Every day, stock your refrigerator with tap water in a pitcher or jug. This will be your first source of water in the event of a disaster. Make a habit of putting water in your coffee maker in the evening. This can help ensure you have additional water supply.
25. **Enjoy a glass of water, right now.** Most of us do not drink enough water. In the case of a survival scenario, most people will be operating at a deficit. You can tip the odds in your favor by quenching your thirst now.
26. **Check on your water supply.** It is recommended to have a minimum of one gallon of water per person per day.

27. **Rotate your canned goods.** Prepare a meal from your stock. Look for dented, rusted, or cans that have bulged, and throw them out.
28. **Assemble something from your emergency equipment.** Take something out of the box and test it. Assemble the camp cooking stove or try out the new solar oven. You may find it is missing a piece or has a broken part or it does not work as well as you thought.
29. **Clean.** There is a or drawer or closet you have been meaning to re-arrange. Take it one drawer, box, shelf, or compartment at a time: you will find you have more space for storage.
30. **Buckets**. Buy extra five-gallon buckets for storage.
31. **Lids**. Buy Gamma Lids to make opening and sealing your buckets easier without a bucket opener.
32. **Check for leaks in your water supplies.** Perhaps you have stacked water too high or notice that a bottle has sprung a leak. Monitoring could save the day. If you neglect your water supplies, the leakage could damage floors and possibly ruin your food sources and other supplies, for example, toilet paper and paper towels.
33. **Learn a new skill.** Preppers always have new skills to master. While you can, go on YouTube and learn as much as you can.
34. **Start chopping firewood.** Your wood must be at least half a year old (preferably a year) to burn effectively. Keeping firewood stocked will be the most difficult part of an off-grid life.
35. **Get a firestarter and practice building a fire.** You will need to stock multiple kinds

of firestarters, to have backups. Starting a fire and keeping it going is not as easy as some think.

36. **Fill your car with gas.** A tank is never more than half empty in a prepper household.
37. **Vehicle**. Keeping vehicles prepared also means having regular maintenance, and checking the oil and water levels.
    a. **Stock up on car maintenance items.** You will always need oil changes, coolants, spark plugs, and air filters. While you are at it, check your spare tires. Stock a fan belt and a timing belt. A tow strap is immensely useful and often overlooked.
38. **Take a hike.** Preppers and their families are in their best possible physical condition because they walk, run, and exercise every day. Do something active with your family to keep in peak shape.
39. **Hygiene**. Poor hygiene in the aftermath of a catastrophe can be one of the biggest killers. To avoid the risk of infections caused by poor sanitation, get your portable toilet set up.
40. **Get to know your neighbors.** Perhaps there is a medical doctor, nurse, or EMT down the street. Ask him or her to review your first aid kit. Dentists and dental hygienists could provide assistance.
41. **Shhhh**. Remember the first rule of Prep Club: do not talk about Prep Club. Be a good neighbor: if you are public about your prepping plans, then you must integrate neighbors in your planning efforts. Help them develop a means of survival.
42. **Read prepper books and articles.** Pick up a book on prepping, like this one. There are

always new ideas to consider for enhancing your prepper lifestyle.

43. **Try out a new prepper recipe.** Make dinner tonight with ingredients from your prepper's pantry and stored water. Now is the time to try a recipe and to calculate how long it will take for you to make that meal using foods in your pantry and using your prepper stove. You may discover that you need some new recipes or to expand the ingredients in your pantry.
44. **Try it.** Live off your freeze-dried foods for a week.
45. **Make it.** Make individual sizes from your freeze-dried food so you can sample a variety. Calculate how much water you will need and how much food you require as a household to feel satiated. Often the recommended serving size on the package will not match your actual needs. You will also quickly discover the need for variety.
    a. With freeze-dried foods, additional water will be needed.
46. **Vaseline**. I wrote a whole chapter on Vaseline, but it is worth mentioning again. Petroleum jelly is an excellent fire-starter when paired with cotton balls. Combined with gauze it is also an effective ointment for scrapes, burns, and cuts for your first aid kit. Additionally, it can soothe chapped lips, and prevent chafing/friction between skin and clothing while walking or running long distances. Vaseline has many uses for preppers.
47. **Learn sign language**. You may find yourself in a situation where communicating with family members covertly will be the best course of action. Practice a few essential signs (made up or

real ones) to help you communicate should marauders threaten your family and supplies.

48. **Clear the condiment shelf of your refrigerator.** While canned foods can last well beyond the "use-by" date, condiments in open bottles can be dangerous to your health. There is no need to store a salad dressing from ten years ago or a hot sauce that is too spicy for your family's tastes. Get rid of them. Use the shelf space for bottled drinks. You can never have enough water stored and this is a way to squeeze in some extra bottles.
49. **Take self-defense classes/tools.** Get some defense tools. Even a simple self-defense key chain, could save your life.
50. **Shop a farmer's market and can something.** Shopping at a local farmer's market supports neighboring families. You might find the perfect ingredients for your home canning or dehydrating projects. Most farmer's markets are organic: a bonus.
51. **Check the sodium content of your canned goods.** FEMA warns that salty foods increase the amount of water you want/need to drink. This extra thirst threatens your water supply by depleting it more quickly than if you had food with lower sodium content.
52. **Add more iodized salt to your shopping list.** Iodine is an essential trace element, and salting is an important task in preserving. Check the label: many salts do not contain iodine.
53. **Stock up on board games, card games, and books.** How will you pass the time with your family when they can no longer watch

TV or look at their smartphones all day? Buy books and games for the holidays and keep them in reserve for the day the lights go out.

54. **Save seeds.** Stockpile seeds for growing produce.
55. **Learn how to read a map and to navigate without a compass.** Figure out how to navigate without a compass. A compass might not work, and GPS may not be available. Also, your bug-out plan should include alternate exit routes.
56. **Tires**. Get products to repair punctures and inflates your tires. Some newer tires can drive over fifty miles with a puncture. If you do not have such tires, you can obtain help from a canned device to inflate your tires. One popular product is "Fix a Flat".
57. **Super-size your food storage.** Super-size your prepping by buying food in bulk and putting it into food-grade buckets. Mylar bags will keep your food safe for the long term. Plastic bags will help protect macaroni and flavored rice products from moisture and vermin; plus, by labeling, you can easily and quickly identify expiration dates.
58. **TP**. Stock up on toilet paper and then get some more. After that, get even more toilet paper.
59. **Cut your old garments.** On the homestead, nothing goes to waste. Cut up your old garments to make rags or towels. These are particularly valuable for use in vehicle repair.
60. **Tarpaulins (Tarps).** Tarps have many uses. Check your tarps to make sure they

are still viable, waterproof, and free of punctures.

a. **A tarp can help you in a pinch.** Tarps have many uses. A tarp can help you temporarily patch a roof. The problem is that ordinary (blue) tarps may attract too much attention. A camouflage tarp will better help you hide many things. Be sure to have enough duct tape, bungee cord, and stakes on hand. And yes, camouflage duct tape can be purchased. Get some camouflage nets, too.

61. **Plywood**. Do you have enough plywood to patch up a broken window or to batten down the hatches in the event of a world in chaos?
62. **Buy non-food supplies at the grocery store.** Toilet paper, paper towels, trash bags, can-opener, and more. (Get manual can openers and spread them among your bug-out and other supplies.) Disposable vinyl gloves for sanitation, and dishwashing gloves to help protect your hands, disinfectant wipes, and freezer bags should be included.
63. **Cash**. Have cash on hand that you can use at the grocery stores when credit cards might not work.
    a. If the electricity goes down, larger stores might not be able to process credit card payments. However, smaller grocery stores may be willing to take cash for your purchases.
64. **Pawn**. Pawn some useless stuff and purchase silver coins or cash. Investing in precious metals could pay off the day the dollar devalues to next to nothing, just the way it did during the Great Depression.

65. **Silver**. Save silver, start collecting nickel and copper too. Find a good spot for safekeeping. Then go through your coins and start sorting the old copper pennies and nickels from the new ones. Nickel and copper have more value than the five-cents (nickel) and penny (copper) the coins with these metals are worth. Likewise, so does the copper penny.
66. **Bake**. Learn to bake bread, cookies, and cakes.
67. **Start a prepper's binder.** Gather all your favorite articles, recipes, instructions, and checklists in one place. This resource will be invaluable.
68. **Review**. Constantly review this book (and others) as you may not have electricity or the Internet.
69. **Review your homeowner's insurance coverage.** Ask your insurance agent to review your policy and advise you on the proper coverage for floods, earthquakes, and other disasters (both manmade and natural).
70. **Stock up on pet supplies.** Prep for a pet, even if you do not have one. Specifically:
    a. Fish antibiotics might be useful for humans when there is no doctor and you cannot get your hands on prescription drugs.
    b. Kitty litter is good for homemade toilets and can get your car out of the snow/ice.
    c. Get dog and cat food for barter
71. **Thermal underwear.** Get some thermal underwear for winter when you may not have heat available.
72. **Clothes**. Check and confirm your bug-out supply of clothes is sufficient.

73. **Get a crank radio.** Information could be the difference between life and death. If you have a crank radio, then you can stay on top of important news. All the power you need to operate this radio is in your hand.
    a. The version I have also has a small solar panel and two flashlights.
74. **Network**. Network with like-minded friends on social media particularly in your area.
75. **Purchase a fire extinguisher and learn how to use it.** I recommend at least one per level in your house and one in each car.
76. **Lice**. Lice will probably be more prevalent if the world goes off-grid. If you do not want exposure to the harsh chemicals of traditional lice treatments, get a lice comb.
77. **Plan for your growing kids.** Buy stuff in advance of kids' growth spurts. For little kids, buy the next size up of diapers, and plan for toddlers.
78. **Shoes.** Set aside sturdy shoes for each of your children in a size larger than they currently use. Garage sales are a great source.
79. **Powdered milk.** Powdered milk is shelf-stable and a good replacement for real milk.
80. **Feminine hygiene.** Stash a large supply of menstrual pads and tampons. They have many uses for survival situations.
81. **Education**. Homeschooling might become necessary, so get some material, and workbooks for a few grades ahead.
82. **Gas mask.** Ensure everyone has the right size gas masks.
83. **Self-defense.** Consider the art of self-defense: both physical and psychological. There is an art to using the right tactics at the right time to defend yourself. Anyone

can avoid, hide and disguise, diffuse, surprise, and retreat.

84. **Scouting**. You are never too old to pick up scouting skills. Pickup a Boy Scout Manual and learn how to “be prepared” the original Boy Scout way. The original aim of Boy Scouts was to promote the ability of boys to do things for themselves and others. They were the original preppers. “Scoutcraft” includes first aid, lifesaving, tracking, signaling, camp craft, woodcraft, chivalry, and patriotism: among other subjects.
85. **Sundial**. Learn to make and read a sundial and educate yourself on how to tell direction by the position of the sun.
86. **Duct tape**. Duct tape is one of the most popular and useful prepper tools. Stock up with as much duct tape as you can.
87. **Dump your Teflon pans and get into cast iron.** Teflon emits toxic particles that can kill birds. Invest in a cast-iron skillet. This will provide a healthy dose of iron and can be used to cook on any kind of heat source. You can place an iron skillet directly on the fire.
88. **Know how to include electrolytes in your cooking.** A pinch of salt, about two tablespoons of honey or sugar, and two cups of water or tea could help restore your electrolyte balance. If available, add the juice from half a lemon.
89. **Learn how to tie knots.** Teach your kids how to tie knots, too. With all the Velcro around, it is an art that has gone by the wayside and yet tying knots is a very useful skill.
    a. Different types of knots will slip or fail if used in the wrong situation.

90. **Prepare for nausea, diarrhea, and upset stomach.** Your diet will certainly change during a survival situation. Plan now for worms, diarrhea, and general stomach upset.
91. **Go for target practice.** Enjoy your Second Amendment and improve your marksmanship. You are only as skilled as your last shooting session.
92. **If you do not like guns,** learn archery or pick up a slingshot and practice.
93. **Eat chocolate and stash some.** Chocolate is an antioxidant and superfood.
94. **Make an extra credit card or mortgage payment.** To reduce debt, start with the smallest card balance and make an extra payment to get that debt paid off. Then work toward your next goal. Ideally, preppers should have no debt.
95. **Distilled water** (the purest form of water). Reconsider your water supply source. Get the facts about your local tap water and consider drinking distilled water and storing it instead of tap water. Learn how to make distilled water, it is not that difficult.
96. **Keep your water supplies off the cement.** Storing water bottles directly on the cement floor of your garage may be dangerous. If the cement heats, which it often does in an unventilated garage space, it may leach chemicals. Store your water on a pallet or platform. Even a plank of plywood is better than nothing.
97. **Check your freeze-dried foods, specifically with respect to your stored water.** On average you will need to store one cup of water for each serving of freeze-dried food.

98. **Take refrigeration seriously**. Clean out your refrigerator and freezer: defrost the later. You may find you have more room than you thought you had.
99. **Make a Zeer pot.** A Zeer pot is a simple refrigeration system that starts with clay pots, sand, and water. The advantage of a Zeer pot is that it does not use electricity. I describe how to make one in my previous book, Doomsday Bunker Book.
100. **Build a Faraday cage.** A Faraday cage is a shielding device intended to protect electronic equipment from intense disruptions caused by solar radiation or an EMP. I describe how to make one in my book, Doomsday Bunker Book.
101. **Turn off the grid.** Have a drill with your family and bug in for the weekend without electricity. Light some candles and see what you learn from a bug-in weekend.
102. **Set up an inventory spreadsheet.** Once you have amassed some supplies, create an inventory list. Soon you will feel better with the knowledge that you have prepped well knowing exactly what you have and what you still need. At the conclusion of this book, I share with you a list of the foods and personal inventory that I use.
103. **Keep quiet.** The first rule of Prep Club is "Do not talk about Prep Club." Avoid the unwanted commentary you will receive from friends and family by simply keeping your prepping secretive. Rest assured; you are not a crazy prepper. People of the past were always preppers. They stockpiled food and supplies for lean times and winter.
104. **Clique**. See if there are other preppers in your area with whom you can network. I

know, "Don't talk about Prep Club." But you will be better prepared with others in your clique.

105. **Nuclear disaster**. Learn what to do in case of a nuclear disaster. I discuss it in my book, Doomsday Bunker Book.
106. Prepare for and practice to bugout
107. Prepare for and practice to bug-in

SAFE ROOM

A safe room is a safe location within a residence or other building. The concept of a safe room is simple, prepare a room within the interior of the home where the family can safely retreat during a threat and safely wait until assistance arrives.

Ideally, it should be a secure room with no exterior walls. If you have the money, put up shielding and insulation on all walls, the floor, and the ceiling. Also, a good idea is to make sure you have plumbing and electricity available. Space for some supplies is also important.

A Safe Room

Pick a room with few, or if possible, no windows. Higher stories are better because chemical agents are heavier than air and fall to the ground. If possible, choose a space with water, a toilet (makeshift if need be), and an electrical outlet. Set aside plenty of duct tape for sealing, doors, windows, and vents. Prepare a seventy-two-hour BOB to store it in the room. Also include inexpensive breathing filters, rated at N95 or better, for each household member.

How to Prepare the Sealed Room

All supplies should already be in the room.

To seal a room in a bio-chemical emergency, first shut off all air intakes into the house (heat, air, attic fans, ceiling fans, etc.). If your home is heated with gas or uses gas appliances, shut it off for safety. Taking your gas mask (and supplies) into the selected room, run the duct tape along all windows where the glass joins the sill, (where the sill meets the frame) and along all window seams and joints.

Completely cover the windows with polyethylene, trash bags, or painter's drop plastic sheeting, or even plastic shower curtains: you can buy these at the dollar store. Anchor these on every side of the wall around the window, and sealing thoroughly with duct tape.

Once all the members of your household have entered the room, complete the sealing using adhesives such as duct, packing, masking or painter's tape between the door and the frame and the frame and walls. The space between the door and the floor should be covered with a towel. Pack the towel firmly. The towel will act as a filter of sorts allowing some air in while filtering the contaminants. Use a bleach/water solution periodically sprayed on the towel under the door if there is a biological threat and vinegar if chemical or just plain water to protect against radioactive dust.

Your room will not be perfectly airtight, but the air intake will be significantly diminished. You do not want your breathing to deplete the oxygen in your safe enclosure which will increase the carbon dioxide.

Ideally, a sealed room has its emergency filter that blocks particles and purifies the air from toxins.

Leave the front door of your house unlocked, to allow rescue units access if needed and available.

Turn on the (ideally hand-cranked) radio to get information from the local authorities about the situation. Wait for an "All clear" from the radio or local municipal rescue/defense. The wait could last for several hours or even days.

Create a Quarantine Room

Use a room separate from your safe room either on the first floor or the foyer area near your front door. Using duct tape and plastic sheeting, as mentioned earlier, seal off the area, excluding the door by which potentially contaminated persons can enter. Place seventy-two hours' worth of food and water along with the means to wash and several trash bags, a change of clothing, and a means to use the toilet, as well as the necessary supplies to re-seal the room.

Once all the supplies are in place, seal it off from the inside and signal the person or persons to enter the quarantine area. Once they are inside direct them to seal their entrance into the room and strip off all clothing and place them in a trash bag. They should then place that trash bag in another one and seal it as well by tying it then taping it shut.

Next, have them wash with soap and water paying extra attention to their hair, placing the dirty water and rags in the makeshift toilet (only if using soap and water).

Never urinate in any solution containing bleach, as a chemical reaction between the ammonia in your urine and chlorine bleach will result creating a toxic chlorine gas that will eat holes in your lungs and kill you in an hour (depending on the concentration of the gas and the size of the quarantine room).

Have them put on the new, clean clothes and get comfortable because they will have to remain there for seventy-two hours before entering the rest of the house with the other occupants, ensuring that they are not infected by a biological agent.

Keep the supplies on hand so you can re-use the quarantine room again if need be.

If it is a radiological threat, once they have washed and changed clothes, they should be able to join the rest of the household. If the threat is radiological, whichever side of the safe room you are using that is closest to an exterior house wall should be layered in radiation shielding material at least three feet high for shelter that you and others can hide behind. This can be made by tipping over your refrigerator, re-positioning your washer and dryer, filling a plastic tub with water, or stacking cases of bottled water (do not drink this water).

Decontaminate Yourself

For radioactive dust or ash

Remove all your clothing and place it in a trash bag, then double seal it in another trash bag and seal that with tape.

Next, scrub yourself with soap and water paying extra attention to your hair and the hairy, exposed parts of your body such as arms, legs, and face. Blow your nose or clean out your nostrils with a tissue.

For a biological agent

Remove all your clothing and place it in a trash bag, sealing it in another bag with tape.

Next, scrub yourself with one-part bleach and ten parts water solution over your entire body paying special attention to your fingernails but not your hair, face, or sensitive areas. For sensitive areas, use soap and water. Blow your nose or clean out your nostrils with a tissue.

For a chemical agent

Remove all your clothing and place it in a trash bag, then place it in another trash bag and seal that with tape.

Next, using either activated charcoal, regular (non-quick lighting) charcoal briquettes (if the agent smells like lighter fluid then do not use it) or crushed wood coals, scrub skin that was exposed to the chemical agent, including your face, neck, and any exposed arms and legs then wash it off with soap and water. Blow your nose or clean out your nostrils with a tissue.

Risk Factors for a Biological Attack

All biological weapons have a high failure rate in terrorist attacks because even though they are quite deadly, dispersal/delivery of them effectively is difficult. Changes in air quality, pH, temperature, and humidity, as well as other changes in the environment (not to mention the life span of the device itself), make efficient delivery of these bacteria and viruses difficult.

For example, anthrax is one-hundred percent deadly when it enters the lungs of human beings. The minimum fatal dose for a person is one anthrax spore.

However, these spores clump together and adhere to dust and dirt particles, which makes them too big to infiltrate the lungs.

Anthrax has a very small rate of "secondary uptake," which means that once it hits the ground, it tends to end its delivery cycle. People who shelter in sealed rooms just wait it out for up to twenty-four hours but then would wait for days to determine if they were infected or not. As long as they remained calm and secluded from infected areas, they should escape infection.

Smallpox is far more persistent, though less deadly, than anthrax with a mortality rate of about thirty-three to sixty-six percent: people at ground zero of an attack would fare the worst. People secure from the initial infection would have to be prepared to quarantine themselves to avoid contact from victims whose symptoms would not appear for several weeks.

A biological weapon could be delivered into the water supply making it a more contagious and aggressive agent. Filtering and water purification in the home can deflect the effectiveness of such an attack; and boiling water for seven minutes would likely kill any biological entity. However, poisoning could still occur and last for several days before symptoms appear. Drinking bottled water or at least boiling all water that comes from the tap (for seven minutes) before you drink it might be a good precautionary step if you fear a biological attack.

Chemical warfare and terrorism are much more likely. Mustard gas canisters can be opened, and their vapors simply allowed to disperse – without explosions, nor bursts of munitions. Their damage would not be known for a couple of days. An unsuspecting and crowded public could suffer catastrophic pain, injury, blindness, and loss of life two or three days after exposure. This is one of the most realistic and horrifying scenarios. Yet it is one that an educated public can prevent.

SAFE ROOM

Do not stand in any area where vapors are escaping. Teach your children not to stand in plumes of smoke or run through any vaporous substance. Iraq used mustard gas in smoke bombs, thus enticing Iranian soldiers to run into the smoke to pursue supposedly retreating enemy soldiers. It was a highly successful ruse.

People in crowded or enclosed places are in the greatest danger of a terrorist chemical agent attack. Granted, a city might just get bombed by chemical warheads, but that scenario is not nearly as likely as a crowded building being sealed off and a chemical agent introduced into the ventilation system.

We know from the Tokyo subway attack[10] that subways, terminals, even trains, and planes are in the most danger of attacks of this nature. As are crowded buildings – especially theaters, which have no windows and are dark.

Many people buy gas masks, but chemical-biological weapons can strike when a gas mask and bio-suit are out of reach.

Remember, as we learned on September 11, 2001, terrorists often like to make grand displays in very public places. So, the answer is to be smarter than our enemies. Avoid crowded and dark, enclosed building interiors that rely heavily on a ventilation system rather than open windows and fresh air. Visit enclosed buildings only when it is necessary, during off-peak hours. For example, go to the mall as soon as it opens in the morning or at around three in the afternoon on weekdays, NOT on Saturdays at noon. Do not go to movies on opening night. If you are in a crowded, enclosed building, always know where the exits are and your paths to reach them. Simply being aware of your immediate environment is always the first good defense.

---

[10] Sarin gas attack in March of 1995 killing twelve and injuring about fifty.

To Bunker or Not

This is a difficult question as bunkers are either expensive or very expensive. The cheap bunkers are not going to do anything except collapse or otherwise prove worthless. I wrote a whole book, Doomsday Bunker Book, which covers the building of either an underground or an aboveground bunker. In my opinion, one of those is going to be your best option. In my above-mentioned book, I talk about many of the common flaws in poorly constructed bunkers so that you can avoid them in yours.

Since building a bunker will be beyond the financial means of many people I will mention a few other options for consideration.

School bus

Some people convert a school bus for use as a bunker. This can work as it is sturdy, well built, and travels well. The problem I have with it is when people burry it. If they are buried just below the surface, that is not deep enough to protect the occupants against chemical or especially nuclear contamination. If they are buried, there is a high risk of collapse from the weight of the dirt.

Using a school bus as a bug-out vehicle may be a good idea to consider.

Shipping container

Shipping containers come in different sizes and are quite versatile and strong. They can be buried, but again, not deep. The perimeter is made to support a significant amount of weight, but when you pile several feet of dirt on top, that can compromise its structural integrity.

I have heard of several instances where shipping containers have collapsed from the weight of the dirt on top of them. If you do want to bury a shipping container or a school bus, build a concrete liner around them with a monolithic dome. See Doomsday Bunker Book for more information about that.

RV or Camper

I like this idea as they have all the comforts of home and can travel well. Unfortunately, they are not built for protection and cannot be buried. They can be quite expensive, but depending on your needs, it might be worth it.

PANDEMIC PREPAREDNESS

A pandemic results from a virus or other-causing pathogen that affects a large number of people in multiple countries. An endemic disease is one that has become long-lasting affecting only a particular people or a certain area. You never know when a pandemic could strike. Oh wait, we are in one right now (at least while I type these words). Were you prepared? Are you prepared?

Prepare now for future pandemics. Remember how crazy things became when the Covid-19 pandemic hit your area? Pandemics can kill quickly and you can get a virus simply by being at the wrong end of a sneeze or by flying in a plane. Yet many people do survive pandemics.

Get your pandemic kit together (suggestions below) or buy a ready-made one. With so many commercially available kits already put together for you, you will know exactly what to do in case of a pandemic emergency. Stock a kit in your car during flu season and you will be ready for the next iteration of the flu virus.

Make sure you are in good health, eat well, and exercise regularly.

Pandemic Mask

One of the most basic things you can do to prepare for a pandemic is to stock up with antiviral masks. While certainly helpful, an antiviral mask does not cover the entire face and provides more protection for the vulnerable (in the case of Covid-19, the elderly for example) than for you. They are inexpensive and effective, but during a pandemic, they will be difficult to come by. Another reason to wear a pandemic mask in crisis is to have a constant reminder not to touch your nose and mouth to avoid contagion.

Consider these basic types of masks.

- Antiviral masks
- N95/N100 mask
- Gas Masks
- Face shield

Goggles

One of the most overlooked items in a pandemic is goggles. You will want to wear goggles during a pandemic, for example, if you are caring for the sick in your home. If someone in the family has been exposed to the virus, you should use goggles.

Their purpose is to help prevent droplets from entering the cavities of the eye. How do droplets get into your eyes? Mostly from fluid in your nose and mouth, but contagion can enter your eyes in any number of ways including:

- Coughs (droplets can stay in the air for forty-five minutes)
- Sneezes (can easily travel about ten feet)
- Blood splashes
- Rubbing your eyes

Duct Tape and Tarp

During a pandemic, preppers must consider quarantine as part of their response plan. Use duct tape and tarps to seal off windows and doorways. Learn how to set up a quarantined safe room elsewhere in this book.

Gloves

There are several types of gloves to consider for pandemic preparedness. Medical gloves have two basic categories, sterile and non-sterile. Sterile gloves are for examining patients and performing surgeries. For pandemic prepping, non-sterile nitrile gloves will suffice.

- **Nitrile exam gloves**. Nitrile is chemical and puncture-resistant providing a level of protection against liquids, gases, and sharp objects. Non-allergenic and non-irritating Nitrile exam gloves are inexpensive. Nitrile exam gloves are latex-free and standard practice in the medical industry.
- **Chemical-resistant gloves**. For pandemics such as Ebola (and other highly contagious and deadly pathogens), you will need a second layer of gloves that have a case-hardened finish that

enhances both chemical and abrasion resistance, such as green chemical resistant gloves. They are loose-fitting.

- **Foodservice gloves**. You will want powder-free food handling plastic gloves to keep your meal prep hygienic. With Coronavirus the incubation period can be long and the food preparer in your family or group may be unaware of his or her illness or be asymptomatic. Plan for such contingencies with food service gloves.

Learn how to properly remove gloves, pulling them inside out and rolling them into each other so the possible bio-hazard virus never touches your skin.

Tyvec, Chemical or Hazmat Suit

Personal protective equipment (PPE) includes a Tyvec suit, also known as a chemical suit or a hazmat suit (short for Hazardous Materials). Tyvec is an impermeable material. Ensure your coveralls protect against substances, including chemicals, biological agents, or radioactive materials.

Buy a hazmat suit for every member of the household and then extras for unexpected guests or new exposures. Besides, it is always a good idea to have backups.

Antiseptics and Disinfectants

Stock a variety of antiseptics and disinfectants for cleaning doorknobs and handles, bathrooms, kitchens, and other shared surfaces.

The difference between an antiseptic and a disinfectant is that antiseptics apply to the skin while a disinfectant is applied to surfaces. The best antiseptic is good old-fashioned soap and water, but when this might not be available, you will need antiseptic wipes on hand.

Antiseptics

- Antiseptic wipes and hand sanitizers will help you control exposure and help minimize the risks of pandemic contamination on your hands; however, unless you are wearing gloves it may be too late if the virus has already made contact with your skin. Other points of entry to the body include the nasal passages, eyes, and ears.
- A good example of an antiseptic is an iodine solution. This first aid antiseptic will help prevent the risk of infection from minor cuts, scrapes, and burns.

Disinfectants

- A disinfectant is a chemical liquid that destroys bacteria, viruses, and fungi on surfaces. A sanitizer performs the same function; however, it is generally safe for food handling. Both kill bacteria and both apply to surfaces.
- Disinfectant wipes are good when you have limited water.
- Food surface sanitizing solutions are disinfectants too.

Stock them all: soaps, sanitizers, and disinfectants.

Liquid Soaps

Washing hands is among the best ways to fight contagion. There is a proper handwashing technique you can learn from the Centers for Disease Control (Wet, Lather, Scrub, Rinse, Dry). This five-point method for effective handwashing is especially important during a pandemic and requires soap.

Stock up on liquid soaps. You can choose antibacterial soaps, but viruses are becoming cleverer and nothing beats lathering up with a good liquid soap. Many viruses live on wet surfaces, which is why you should not rely on bar soaps that stay moist.

Antiviral Facial Tissues

For a respiratory pandemic, facial tissues are a "must-have" on your supply list. The best kind of tissue to buy are anti-viral ones.

Thermometers

Fever is a symptom of many illnesses. There are multiple kinds of thermometers you should stock for different circumstances.

- **Analog thermometer**. An analog thermometer can help you during an ElectroMagnetic Pulse (EMP), or simply when your batteries drain from a digital thermometer.
- **Disposable thermometer**. Have disposable thermometers handy in your bugout bag (not in a car as heat can ruin them). These are good for using on other people about whom you are not sure of their health status.
- **No-touch thermometer**. No-touch thermometers were used extensively in Ebola-stricken countries. They are also good when

you do not want to have physical contact with someone when you do not know their health status.

Medicine

Ensure your medicine cabinet is well stocked. When a pandemic hits, these supplies will be among the first to become unattainable.

Check my first aid list toward the end of this book.

It is also a good idea to have a stock of your prescription medications. Talk to your primary care physician about how to safely go about this.

Electrolytes

Another important and often overlooked supply item for a pandemic, such as Coronavirus, are electrolytes, which are required for bodily functions, including muscle function. Electrolytes include bicarbonate, calcium, chloride, magnesium, phosphate, and sodium.

Ensure your overall prepper supply list includes plenty of emergency drinks that contain electrolytes. It would be a good idea to learn how to make electrolytes and I describe it elsewhere in this book.

Bio-Hazard Bags

A bio-hazard bag provides a high-density isolation liner to provide maximum film strength for tough applications. They also feature star seal bottoms which allow equal weight distribution and leak resistance. To warn others, bags are red to indicate the use of infectious waste or hazardous waste.

The red infectious waste bags, are for the collection of materials that might be contagious and should be burned when full.

Diapers (Adult and Kids)

Family members of cancer patients and some stricken with dementia can appreciate more than most the necessity for adult diapers. Containing the mess avoids unsanitary conditions and reduces the spread of disease. Cloth diapers serve as a first-aid item for stopping bleeding, and you can use them to clean up vomit or provide a cool water compress for a fever.

I prefer to have both disposable and cloth diapers on hand.

Vomit Bags (Emesis Bags)

Single-use emesis bags will help with sickness cleanup. This product can be difficult to find.

Laundry Detergent

You will need to clean and sterilize bedding or throw it away. Washing laundry on the sanitary (deep clean) setting is imperative. If you do not, you will recontaminate yourself and continue to spread the virus.

Portable Radio

As with any massive catastrophe, your list of pandemic supplies should include communications. A portable radio might just save your life. As mentioned herein, I recommend a hand-crank radio.

Water Filtration System

Water could also contain contaminants that can lead to illness or worse. Even if the water is not the cause of sickness, the fact remains that the entire water supply could be stopped if the municipal water supply cannot operate properly due to the illness or confinement of maintenance staff. Having the means to filter water would put your survival at better odds. Get your water storage and filtration system in place now while there is still time.

Survive a Pandemic

In the event of a pandemic alert, the following is a list of suggestions for you and your family to follow. Mind you this list goes to extremes, but you will need to take such measures to survive a pandemic.

- **Stock up on supplies while they are still available.** Ensure you have the items described in this book to help you prepare for a pandemic.
- **Take Probiotics.** Improve your family's intestinal flora now and especially during an outbreak. Have plenty of probiotics on hand and increase your intake of probiotics in supplements and in the foods you eat, like acidophilus in kefir and yogurts. Eat well, including a healthy diet of fresh fruits and vegetables.
- **Reduce your dependency on antibiotics.** Antibiotics are overused in the United States and this compounds the problem of adaptive micro-organisms. Talk to your physician about going without antibiotics.
- **Get a survival prescription.** Consider getting a flu vaccine.

- **Do not touch stuff others touch.** Avoid as much as possible contact with pencils and pens, elevator buttons, doorknobs, coins, handrails, and places many other hands have touched, particularly during the flu season.
- **Avoid shaking hands.** During flu season, tell others that you are not shaking hands. Do not worry about being rude: it is your life.
- **Wash your hands frequently.** Before eating and after having been out and about, make it a routine to wash your hands with hot water and clean under the fingernails. Recite the alphabet or sing "happy birthday" twice and you will have washed your hands for an adequate time.
- **Minimize spreading sickness from sneezes and coughs.** Cover your mouth when you sneeze to avoid spreading droplets. Turn your body away from someone coughing or sneezing.
- **Avoid touching your face (eyes, nose, and mouth).** Humans tend to touch their face six times every few minutes. That is one of the fastest ways to contract any contagion.
- **Stay away from people.** Just stay home during an extreme outbreak. Do not send the kids to school. Do not go to work. If you can, because you stocked up, do not go to the grocery store.
- **Wear a NIOSH-95 Respirator (pandemic mask).** If you must venture out and expose yourself and your family during a pandemic or an extreme crisis, then wear your mask.
- **Wear your Tyvec suit, gloves, and goggles.** This is in the case of an extreme situation.
- **Quarantine your family.** Set up a quarantine room if you suspect a family member is sick or has been exposed during a pandemic outbreak.
- **Take notes.** Keep a record of diarrhea, vomiting, coughing, breathing problems, and rashes of anyone in your care, so that you can

report to medical staff if necessary. Make sure to mark the date and time, along with the severity of the problem. In this way, you can monitor the progress of the illness.

- **Get information.** Check the websites or phone the Centers for Disease Control and the World Health Organization for important alerts and information.
- **Expect disruptions in utilities.** As people stop showing up for work, the mechanical equipment behind the grid will weaken and may eventually fail. You may as well expect the unexpected.
- **Be alert about pneumonia.** You may well survive a pandemic and yet succumb to the secondary problem of a pneumonia infection. At-risk groups include people more than sixty-five, people with diabetes, asthma, and other chronic illnesses.
- **Misc.** Before a pandemic strikes, assuming you have enough warning because it started elsewhere, consider doing the following things:
    - Laundry
    - Change and wash your linens
    - Clean your carpets
    - Sanitize your doorknobs
    - Have your vehicle detailed
    - Do a complete inventory of your supplies
    - Check up on family members

Pandemic Scenario

I write this book as the Coronavirus, or Covid-19 is still going on and the rioting and looting are continuing. Where I am sitting and typing this manuscript, we are still in lockdown. I am not going to go into the politics of the situation and ask questions like did we do enough? Did we do too much?

Should we have done this or that? Etc. That is not my concern, I am just here to look at what you and I can do to prepare ourselves for a future event.

A pandemic can quickly cause services to be shut down as people huddle at home or the hospital. The domino effect will be in effect. People will flock to hospitals and care facilities for real or imagined problems. Some of the hospital staff will bring home the pandemic; whether it is the medical staff, the food, the janitorial, or administrative staff. Many will choose to stay at home rather than risk their lives. Gas stations could shut down as employees no longer return to work.

The store shelves will be empty as trucks will not have enough gas to deliver groceries. Employees will not be available to load or unload trucks even if there were enough gas. Maybe the truck drivers will be sick. Soon water and electricity will halt as the grid shuts down due to lack of manpower.

Prices of products will have increased manifold while people panic and stores raise their prices exorbitantly.

Toilet paper and paper towels will not be available for purchase at any price. Prices of foods will easily double in price as it will be difficult or impossible to get product to the stores.

People will riot and loot.

You are forewarned and hopefully fore-armed.

Be safe.

CAR SURVIVAL KIT

You spend a significant amount of time in your car commuting to work or school, running errands, traveling on vacations, and weekends. If catastrophe strikes, big or small, you can be ready with a survival kit for your car.

With a well-equipped kit in your car, you can have virtually everything you might need to survive. Begin with a sturdy utility box or toolbox. Make space under the car seat, in the trunk, or tucked in the glove compartment or the seat pockets for “must-haves”.

The following is a list of essential things to keep in your vehicles for survival, so you are ready for bugging out. These items will also help you in case you are caught in a storm and cannot get home.

Containers, Filters, and Tablets

When building your car emergency kit, remember to pack water. Many preppers will stock up in their homes plenty of water but forget to put any in their vehicles. Always carry water in your ride, along with ways to purify water in case you get stuck somewhere.

- **Water.** Always carry fresh water with you.
- **Metal water container.** With a metal water container, you can boil water if need be. The metal water container will also be useful if you pack food, which you can cook.
- **Water purification tablets.** Potable Aqua tablets will help you source water in an emergency.
- **Water straw filter.** This is a must in any kit.

Fire Starter

A fire starter should be part of your everyday carry. You should have at least three methods available to you, for example:

- Fire striker
- Hurricane matches make another good everyday carry for your car.
- BIC lighters are dependable fire starters

Knife

It is always a good idea to have a knife on hand for its myriad uses. The knife I keep on me at all times has a glass break on one end to enable me to get out of a car. If in a situation far from home with only one tool, I would want it to be my knife.

Emergency Blanket or Bivy

Winterize your car with a wool blanket ready for emergencies. For trauma, shock or fire, or snow and ice conditions, an emergency blanket is essential, and wool is even better. At a minimum, vehicles should contain a Mylar blanket, which can fold flat and be stored in the glove compartment:

- **Bivy.** A bivy is a lightweight sleeping bag designed to retain body heat and is an absolute necessity when traveling in snow or cold weather.
- **Emergency blanket.** A quality emergency blanket is made of a flame retardant woolen fabric. Because of the moisture and oils present in wool fiber, when exposed to a flame, wool fabric self-extinguishes and turns to ash.
- **Mylar blanket.** The most economical option is a Mylar blanket. It is also a space saver. Mylar blankets have many survival purposes. Include one in your car kit and another in your bugout bag. Ensure you have several Mylar blankets: one for each passenger seat in your vehicle. One Mylar can be used for the ground to prevent dampness and another to help retain body heat.
- **Heavy-duty garbage bag.** Even a trash bag can help you retain warmth in an emergency and is considered the poor man's bivy. A trash bag is also convenient as a biohazard bag.
- **Hand warmers.** Be sure to add hand warmers to your kit, particularly if you live or drive in snow regions.

Car Escape Tools

It is natural for preppers to think about "Getting out of Dodge," but what if a prepper's survival depends on getting out of a Dodge (or a Ford, Toyota, or Jeep, etc.). Entrapment is an everyday survival concern and can easily be mitigated with access to the proper tools.

Stow the car escape tool in your car's center console. It is a lifesaver that cuts the seatbelt and breaks windshield glass to enable you to escape your vehicle.

- **Life Hammer.** Escape entrapment in your car with a Life Hammer Escape tool. Its double-sided, steel hammerhead breaks through car windows. Life Hammer's razor-sharp blade cuts easily through safety belts. It includes a mounting bracket for installation and costs about $20.
- **Ranger Rescue Entry Tool.** The Ranger Rescue Entry Tool is a professional-grade tool that combines the functionality of five separate devices into one universal head design. The Ranger Rescue Entry Tool has an ax, pry bar, hydrant wrench, gas shut off, and spanner wrench (for 2 ½" hoses and water mains). This tool is a necessity for all emergency and rescue professionals, and a real luxury for preppers. It weighs 6.35 pounds. Be prepared for anything, even self-defense with this tool if you have extra room to store it. Costs about $330.
- **Tow strap.** Get yourself unstuck with a tow strap that can help you tow 10,000 pounds, which is more than strong enough to extract most vehicles from a ditch or rough spot.

Gas Siphon and a Gas Can

Do not worry that a gas siphon is an item for petty criminals. A siphon pump is a good item to carry with you on your travels in good times and in bad. Good Samaritans exist and may allow you to pump a bit of their gas into your car should you need it. You can worry later about the unethical dilemmas you may face in uncertain times when gas is difficult to secure (and you have the means to obtain some). Also, carry a gas can. It is unwise and unsafe to carry gasoline in an open container.

- **Gas siphon.** Experts caution against the unsafe practice of siphoning gasoline by mouth, warning specifically, that it can result in loss of life. Do NOT siphon by mouth, use a pump.
- **Gas can.** Most spills happen when tipping a normal can to get the spout into the tank opening before the liquid comes out or removing the spout from the target vessel before overflowing. The No-Spill spout is fully in your control, so you tip the can vertical, insert the spout into the vessel opening, then press the button to begin and control pouring. To stop pouring just release the button. It practically eliminates spills and overflows.

Cash

The electricity may be out and having cash to buy the necessities could mean the difference between life and death. Think for example of being in a pharmacy trying to get a vital prescription, or at a gas station and all you have is a useless credit card, but a hurricane is headed your way. The importance of having cash on hand and in your car is essential.

You can hide money in the crevices of your vehicle. Just make sure that your hiding spot is not found by the mechanics and auto-detailers who may have access to your ride.

Wheels or Walking Shoes

Preppers always have a contingency plan for getting home or, "Getting out of dodge." In case your car will not start, or in case all cars will not work, as with an EMP, you will need to stow wheels and/or good walking shoes. Proper navigation is essential, so have a compass and a map on hand as well as some of the following:

- Fold-up bike
- Scooter
- Skateboard
- Roller skates
- Skis
- Snowshoes
- Walking shoes
- Running shoes

You will not want to walk to safety in flip flops, sandals, or high heels in case debris is blocking the way. A pair of sturdy and comfortable old shoes or boots in your car will provide a means of hiking long distances, should you be unable to take public transportation or your car to safety. Old shoes have the benefit of being less likely to blister, but just in case, add moleskin to your car kit.

First Aid Kit

Be equipped to deal with an accident or minor mishap by having a first aid kit handy. Check out my first aid kit supplies list.

Food and Snacks

Ensure you have some food in your vehicle and a folding stove or other means to cook.

- **MREs**. For long trips, it is imperative to pack Meals Ready to Eat, or freeze-dried foods with a means to cook them. Even for short trips, you may like the added security of these foods on your journey. The advantage of MREs is you do not need to bring extra water or a stove to cook them – the flameless heater uses any kind of water whether it is potable or not.
- **Snacks.** Beef Jerky is a great item to stock in the car, but do not stop there. Dried fruits and nuts are a wonderful addition (provided there are no allergies). Protein and energy bars are also good options.
- **Hard candy.** The sugar in hard candy provides excellent quick energy, which you may need if you are stuck on the road.
- **Chewing gum.** Gum provides a stress release and helps aid concentration. The sweetness boost is also a morale booster. In a car emergency, you can use the gum for temporary repair of a radiator to plug a leaky hose. You can also use gum as catfish bait.
- **5-Hour energy drink.** At only two ounces it goes down quickly. A 5-hour energy drink has zero sugar, zero herbal stimulants, and only four calories (depending on the brand). It is packed with B-vitamins, amino acids,

nutrients, and as much caffeine as a cup of coffee. That will get you going if you need to escape on foot.

Tarp or Camouflage

The time may come when it is best to go undetected. With a little advanced planning, you can hide in plain sight using special netting designed to make your car look like it is part of Mother Nature. Purchase enough to cover your vehicle, then make sure to add local foliage to enhance the look.

Power Inverter

Turn the DC from your vehicle into AC for your survival and communications gadgets. It is the next best thing if you do not have a generator.

Shovel

A folding shovel is an essential hand tool for any prepper whether at home, camping, or on the road.

A shovel can help you dig an emergency latrine or serve as an improvised weapon. It is small enough to toss in your bugout bag without weighing you down. Besides its digging abilities, it can operate as a hammer; an ideal option for pounding in tent stakes. Depending on the shovel you purchase, it may have other built-in tools.

Sanitary Supplies

Personal emergencies happen. Even if you do not have room for a portable toilet, pack the sanitation essentials in your car for proper sanitation, including:

- Toilet paper
- Facial tissues
- Paper towels
- Hand wipes
- Hand sanitizers
- Sanitary napkins (they also come in handy for first aid)
- Plastic bags for disposal of waste and to protect your supplies. The bag itself may prove useful for survival to collect water.

Communications

I prefer a hand-cranked radio with NOAA band. Also have your cell phone charged, a spare external cell phone battery, and a car charger. Get your HAM (Amateur) radio license.

Fire Extinguisher

A fire extinguisher can save your life, it has saved mine.

Car Repair Kit

A car repair kit is an essential item. Look for one that contains a voltage tester, bit driver, slip joint plier, drive ratchet handle, driver extension bar, adjustable wrench, spark plug socket, adapter, cable ties, SAE Hex keys, drive sockets, and bits.

Air Pump

To pump your tires in case of a flat you will want an air pump. Get a kit that plugs into your car's cigarette lighter socket. It is also a good idea to get a tire repair kit to fix flats.

MY TRUSTY KNIFE
A BRIEF TALE OF SURVIVAL

If I were in a situation with only one tool with me, it would be my trusty knife. The one I use is a four-inch Marine-style folding knife. I keep it sharp at all times and do not go anywhere without it. It has served me well over the years.

I will share with you a somewhat hypothetical situation where I was dropped off one morning in a remote forest with nothing more than the clothes on my back and my knife. Okay, there was also a large flowing stream nearby with fish. What follows are some of the things I did to survive for a week alone in the woods.

The first thing I did was to take a deep breath of the fresh air and soak up the beauty of nature. It was wonderful. Then I got to the task of looking for food. Looking around there were plenty of edible plants, but

MY TRUSTY KNIFE

I wanted to see if I could catch some fish for dinner to add to what I could to my diet.

To that end, I took some vines to use as a fishing line. Using my knife, I found some small sticks and whittled out a small hook for each line. I dug up some worms to use as bait. Spaced a few dozen yards apart, I set up three of these in the stream (this took about an hour) then headed off to my next task.

The next thing I did was to set a shelter up from the water. I took two branches that were as straight as I could find and made an inverted "V" and tied them together using some vine. Then I tied a long straight branch to its top and secured the other end to a tree. (Imagine, if you will, the beginnings of a pup tent.)

Using more vines, I tied up more branches horizontally along the two long sides of my shelter. Once all that was done, I grabbed handfuls of leaves and other natural debris and covered the two sides of my shelter. The top point was about four feet off the ground and about the same width on the ground. The front was open, and I closed off the back as best as I could using the same method I used for the sides.

For bedding, I stuffed the inside of my shelter with dead leaves, then would wiggle in, feet first, into the pile of leaves. Some of the leaves would act as a mattress and some as a blanket.

All this took several hours.

My next job had to be getting water as I was thirsty. I saw some grapevines in the distance, so I cut one and drank enough to quench my thirst. The advantage of grapevine liquid is that it does not need to be filtered and is high in nutrients. Besides, it tastes great!

I was hesitant to drink from the stream as I had no idea about the cleanliness of the water. I could use it for washing and hygiene, but I was not going to drink it unless I was desperate. However, I was planning to make a filtrations system later.

I cut and peeled the bark from around a tree enabling me to form something of a container by pinching the corners. I held the corners together by partially splitting a small stick to use like a clothespin at each corner. The next day, I would make several more of these containers.

I let the water from the grapevine drip into the container as I went to my next step.

About five or six feet in front of the opening of my shelter I cleared an area with a radius of about six feet of anything that could catch fire. I put a few rocks together to form a semi-circle with the opening toward my shelter.

I gathered tinder, kindling, and wood for my fire and then set out to start it.

Using my knife, I cut a groove in a branch to make a fireboard. Then I whittled down another stick to be my spindle. I set the spindle in the groove and rubbed it up and down the fireboard. I had a small nest of tinder (pine needles and bark shavings) at one end of the fireboard so the embers plowed into it as I was rubbing the spindle back and forth. Eventually, I had a gentle glow that led to a fire.

It took about an hour and a half to get a good fire going.

I was hungry and thankfully, I had one fish on a hook. The other two fishing lines were empty. While the fish was cooking on my fire, I foraged around for berries, lilies, black locust, and anything else I could eat. I finished the water I was able to harvest from the grapevine.

Dinner was delicious and filling. Because I had no real refrigeration, I could not leave anything for the following day. If I had a sealed container like a mason jar, I could have stored food in the stream to keep it fresh.

MY TRUSTY KNIFE

It was a productive day. Before I went to sleep, I fed the fire and enjoyed the feeling of a day well spent. I crawled into the bed of leaves so that some were on top of me and some underneath me.

More tomorrow.

The next day I was awakened by the mellifluous sounds of nature. I would love to have slept in, but I had plenty to do. In this type of situation, one needs to be prepared to work constantly or starve.

The first thing I did was to gather some of the charcoal from the fire ring for later use. Then I tended the fire so I would have it going all day long. I am not a fan of making a fire from sticks: I would prefer to keep what I have going all day rather than start a new one.

I found some flat rocks and used some small sticks and vine to make a few traps for small animals. I placed the traps some distance from my campsite. That took me about two hours total.

I reset the fishing lines and then had a light lunch and relaxed for a bit. I planned to be here for a week, and I wanted to have a few creature comforts.

I used my knife to peel more tree bark and made a few more bowls. Then I made a makeshift spoon from a stick.

Using some of the peeled bark, I made a funnel. At the bottom of the funnel, I put a piece of material that I cut from the bottom of my shirt.

Into the funnel, I placed some crushed charcoal (from my fire), then some sand from the stream, and finally some pebbles. Now I had a homemade water filter and felt more comfortable drinking the water from the stream. The grapevines did not supply me with enough liquid for my drinking needs.

I am not going to bore you will the details of what I did every day, but I will share with you a few of the things

I did over the next week. Of course, every day I had to forage, hunt, and fish for food. I also had to refresh my water filter a few times.

Every day I had to find and cut wood for my fire. To cut wood, I positioned a branch horizontal between two trees as a fulcrum and bent the branch across it to break it.

The biggest project I undertook was to make a bush-craft table. It took me several days and a significant amount of patience. I used branches and vines to make the table at which I could eat and do other preparations.

I also expanded my shelter to give me a small area in front for sitting. Add my table and I had a great place to eat.

On my second day, I also made a couple of spears for self-defense. I do not have the knowledge or skills to make a bow and arrow, but that would have been nice.

I do not like the feeling of a dirty mouth and I take oral hygiene seriously. I had no toothbrush with me, so I made one. I found a short hardwood twig and pounded the end against a rock, which frayed the end. I used pine needles as a toothpick.

I had plenty of food, water, and plant life. Sometimes my traps bore fruit, most of the time not. I did not starve.

My shelter kept me dry on the one day that it rained. The only problem with the rain is that it put out my fire. Since I read plant life (curling of certain leaves and closing of flower petals) I knew that it was going to rain, I was able to protect some wood under my table and in the sitting area.

I had a wonderful time and it was a great learning experience.

CHECKLISTS

In the following chapters, I will share with you some of the checklists that I use. I put these together over the course of several years. Please modify them for your personal needs.

EDC CARRY LIST

Air Filter Mask
Batteries
Blankets
Bug Spray
Carabiner
Chapstick
Chargers
Coffee Filters
Compass
Cotton Balls
Duct Tape
Ear Plugs
Energy Bars
Flashlight
First Aid Kit
Fishing Kit
Fire Starter
Gloves
Glow Sticks
GORP
Hand Sanitizer
Hand Warmers
Hatchet (with a hammer)
Head Lamp
Knives
Lighter
Magnifier
Matches
Meds
Mirror
MREs
Multi-Tool
Nails
Paracord
Pencil & Eraser
Pillow
Poncho
Pot/Pans
Rice
Safety Pins
Saw (folding)
Seasonings
Sewing Kit
Sharpening Stone
Soap
Sponge
Sporks
Steaks
Survival Pen
Tarp (10X10)
Ties (plastic zip ties)
Tin Foil
Tinder
Towel
Toilet Paper
Under Clothes
Water Bag
Water Filter
Whistle
Wipes
Woodstove
Zip Lock Bags

EMERGENCY PREP LIST

The following checklist is what I use at my bug-out location when I know there is a storm coming or some other significant event. I have a modified list that I use at home, but the essentials are the same. Not all items on this list need to be done for every storm or emergency.

Review this list, or your version of it, often to ensure that you are ready for emergencies.

Outside

Ash Container[11]
Blackwater Hose
Check and Fill Generators
Check Pipe Insulation[12]
Check Solar Batteries
Check Solar Panels
Close and Lock Garage
Deploy Security Measures
Driveway Alarm
Fill Vehicle Gas Tanks
Firepits, Clean and Prepare
Galley Hose
Gas Cans, Fill
Ice Melt
Lock Vehicles
Outhouse
Propane Stock
Rocket Stove
Secure Skirt Around Camper
Secure Tarps
Security Cameras
Snow Shovels
Snowblower
Trash
Watershed[13]
Woodshed
Workbench Area

Vestibule

Bring in Plants
Bring in Wood
Check Knives
Extension Cords
Heaters
Load Guns and Clips
Oven
Secure Plastic

[11] I use ash from my fireplace to help melt snow, for traction, odor, cover tracks and more.
[12] During the winter to prevent freezing.
[13] For the water pump, pressure tank, tools and extra water.

Secure Vestibule
Secure Weapons
Under-Camper Lights
Weather Station
Woodstove – Check & Fill

Water

Check Blue Water Barrels
Check Water Bottle Supply
Check Water Pressure Tank
Check Well
Empty Black Water Tank
Empty Galley Water Tank
Empty Gray Water Tank
Fill 7-Gallon Water Tanks
Fill All Water Containers
Fill Animal Water Containers
Fill Freshwater Tank
Make Ice
Put Ice Packs in Freezers
Turn Down Freezers
Water Collection Containers

Charge

Batteries
Cell Phones
Computers
Flashlights
HAM Radio
Hand-Crank Radio
Tablets

Inside

A/C or Heaters
Check First Aid Supplies
Check Food Supplies
Check Medicine Supply
Check & Distribute Flashlights
Check Go-Bags
Check News
Check Prepper Pantry
Check Weather
Clothes Washed
Dishes Washed
Distribute Weapons
Empty De-Humidifiers
Faraday Cages
HAM Radio
Pet Food and Meds
Showers
Toilet Paper
Turn Off Computers
Unplug everything possible
Put All Electronics in Faraday Cage

Food to Make

Hardboiled Eggs
Tuna
Rice
Bread
Soup
Popcorn
Cake

Food to Buy

Bread
Eggs
Fruit
Vegetables

FIRST AID SUPPLY LIST

This list is culled mostly from the Red Cross. I suggest some additional items based on personal experience.

Whether you buy a first aid kit or put one together, make sure it has all the items you may need. My kits have more than double what is on this list. I have kits in each of the cars, the house, bugout location, and buried.

Include any personal items such as medications and emergency phone numbers and any other items your health-care provider recommends. I also suggest having a note from your doctor noting any prescriptions you take, or maybe copies of the scripts of these medications. In this way, you will be able to get refills if necessary, assuming pharmacies are open.

Check the kits regularly. Check expiration dates and replace any used or out-of-date contents.

Quan	Item
1	3-inch gauze roll bandage
2	Absorbent compress dressings (5 x 9 inches)
	Acetaminophen

25	Adhesive bandages (assorted sizes)
1	Adhesive cloth tape (10 yards x 1 inch)
1 roll	Adhesive tape
	Alcohol wipes
5	Antibiotic ointment packets (1 gram @)
3	Antibiotic ointment packs, Triple (0.5g each)
	Anti-diarrheal medications
5	Antiseptic wipes
	Antiseptic solution (like hydrogen peroxide)
5	Antiseptic wipe packets
2	Aspirin packets (81 mg each)
	Bandage, elastic
2	Bandages, elbow and knee plastic (2" x 4")
1	Bandage, Fingertip
1	Bandage, roller (4 inches wide)
	Blanket
1	Breathing barrier for CPR
	Calamine lotion
2	Cold compress, instant
	Cold remedies
	Cough suppressants
1	Emergency blanket
	Eyewash
	Fever reducer
1	First-aid manual
1	Flashlight and extra batteries
2 pair	Gloves, nonlatex
2	Hydrocortisone ointment packets (1 gram @)
	Hydrocortisone cream (1%)
	Ibuprofen
	Pain relievers
	Safety pins
	Saline solution
1	Snake Bite kit
1	Scissors
	Soap
1	Splint
5	Sterile gauze pads (3" x 3")
5	Sterile gauze pads (4" x 4")
	Sterile gauze pads of different sizes
1	Thermometer

FIRST AID SUPPLY LIST

1	Tick removal tool
2	Triangular bandages
1	Tweezers

Other Items to Consider

- Diabetic supplies
- Glasses (extra pair)
- Contacts and solutions
- Neosporin
- Compound W
- Preparation H
- Lice kit
- Burn kit
- Allergy relief
- Back brace
- Stethoscope
- Blood pressure monitor
- Hydrogen peroxide
- Glucose tester
- Epinephrine
- Suture kit
- Antacid
- Moisturizer
- Chapstick
- Vick's Vapo Rub
- Tums

Iodine is an excellent survival tool that comes in handy for several reasons.

- Iodine added to water requires thirty minutes if it is warm and an hour if it is hot outside to sterilize the water.
- Iodine can be used as a first-aid antiseptic. 2% USP helps prevent infections of skin from minor cuts, scrapes, and burns. You need about ten drops per gallon.
- Iodine is a poison if not used in proper proportions.

MY MEDICAL HISTORY

I maintain a chart of my complete medical history as far back as I can recall. I have this in a looseleaf binder and keep it with me at all times. When I go to the doctor or if I need to go to the hospital, all the information is available and accessible to medical personnel. In the binder, I also have copies of all my prescriptions, my driver's license, and insurance cards.

My Personal Information

Name
Address
Phone number
Email address

Business Information
Name
Address
Phone Number
Email address

Emergency Contacts

NAME	PHONE	RELATIONSHIP
		Spouse
		Father
		Mother
		Brother
		Sister

MY MEDICAL HISTORY

Permission is hereby given to speak with XXX about anything involving my condition and treatment. If I am incapacitated, s/he has permission to make all decisions about my care. If s/he is not available, XXX is my second choice, and s/he has permission to make all decisions about my care.

Master Contact List

NAME	ADDRESS	PHONE	FAX	SPECIALTY
				Pharmacy
				PCP
				Dentist
				Cardiologist
				Eye Dr.
				Retinal Dr.
				Mental Health
				Colonoscopy
				Sleep Care
				Durable Equipment

Medicines and Supplements

MEDICATION	FOR	DOSAGE	WHEN

Notes

Allergies

Family History

Current Conditions

Medical Procedures

FOOD INVENTORY

Take an inventory of your stock (food and supplies) every month. Make sure it is increasing in size and quantity and that none of it has expired or spoiled.

The following lists show what I stock. Please modify them for your own needs and household. Remember, only stock what you use and eat and use/eat what you stock.

Date Checked ___________ By Whom ___________________

CANNED

ITEM	
Asparagus	
Beans	
Carrots	
Corn	
Fruit, Mixed	
Jalapeno Tea	
Pears	
Peaches	
Peas	
Pineapple, Chunks	
Pineapple, Crushed	
Pizza Sauce	
Sauce	
Spinach	
Tomatoes	
Tomato Paste	
Tomato Sauce	
Vegetables, Mixed	
Vegetables, Stir Fry	

CONDIMENT

ITEM	
A1 Steak Sauce	
BBQ Sauce	
Honey	
Ketchup	
Maple Syrup	
Mayonnaise	
Mustard	
Mustard, Gray Poupon	
Mustard, Honey Mustard	
Mustard, Whole Grain	
Pickled Ginger	
Salad Dressing	
Sesame Seeds	
Soy Sauce	
Tartar Sauce	

DEHYDRATED

ITEM	
Apple	
Banana	
Carrots	
Chicken	
Dates	
Mashed Potatoes	
Meat	
Onions	
Pineapple	
Potato	
Prune	
Salmon	
Sweet Potato	
Tomatoes	

DESERTS

ITEM	
Apple Butter	
Baker's Chocolate	
Blueberry Pie Filling	
Cherry Pie Filling	
Chocolate Chips	
Chocolate Shells	
Chocolate Spread	
Coconut, Shredded	
Cookies	
DH Brownie	
DH Lemon Supreme	
Graham Cracker Piecrust	
Jelly, Grape	
Jelly, Mango	
Jelly, Strawberry	
Lemon Pie Filling	
M&M'S	
Marshmallow Fluff	
Pudding	
Shortening	
Sprinkles	
Syrup	
Vanilla Wafers	

DRINKS

ITEM	
Apple Juice	
Beer	
Coffee	
Condensed Milk	
Cranberry Juice	
Creamer	
Energy Drink	
Grape Juice	
Hemp Milk	
Hot Chocolate	
Lemonade Powder	
Pineapple Juice	
Powdered Milk	
Rice Milk	
Soy Milk	
Tang	
Tea, Arizona	
Tea Bags	
V8	
Water	
Wine, Red	
Wine, White	

FISH

ITEM	
Mackerel	

Salmon	
Sardine	
Tuna, Chunk	
Tuna, White	

GRAINS

ITEM	
Baked Beans	
Barley	
Black Beans	
Beans	
Buckwheat	
Bulgur	
Corn Meal	
Flour	
Flour, Potato	
Flour, Whole Wheat	
Garbanzo Beans (bags)	
Garbanzo Beans (cans)	
Harvest Blend	
Lentils	
Oatmeal	
Quinoa	
Rice	
Rice, Basmati	
Rice, Brown	
Rice, Jasmine	
Rice, Sushi	
Rice, Wild	
Split Peas	
Vital Gluten	
Yeast	

HEALTH

ITEM	
Flaxseed	

Hemp Protein	
Nori	
Spirulina	
Wakame	

MEALS

ITEM	
Beef and Broccoli	
Cereal	
Chicken and Broccoli	
Egg Substitute	
Egg Whites	
Farina	
MRE, Chicken	
MRE, Meat	
MRE, Vegetarian	
Mu Shu	
Pancake Mix	
Shakshuka	
Sloppy Joe Mix	

OILS

ITEM	
Canola Oil	
Coconut Oil	
Cooking Spray	
Olive Oil	
Peanut Oil	
Sesame Oil	
Soybean Oil	
Sunflower Oil	
Vegetable Oil	

PASTA

ITEM	
Bow Ties	
Lasagna	
Linguine	
Macaroni	
Mac & Cheese	
Matzah	
Orzo	
Spaghetti	
Textured Vegetable Protein	

SEASONING

ITEM	
10X Sugar	
Almond Extract	
Baking Powder	
Baking Soda	
Basil	
Bay Leaf	
Breadcrumbs	
Celery Seed	
Chili Powder	
Cinnamon	
Corn Starch	
Cumin	
Dill	
Duck Sauce	
Food Coloring	
Garlic Powder	
General Tso Sauce	
Italian Seasoning	
Lemon Juice	
Liquid Amino Acid	
Marinara Sauce	
Matzah Meal	
Minced Onion	
Mint	
Mrs. Dash	
Mu Shu Sauce	
Old Bay	
Oregano	
Peanut Sauce	
Paprika	
Parsley	
Pepper	
Potato Starch	
Relish	
Rosemary	
Salt	
Salt, Kosher	
Salt, Popcorn	
Seasoned Salt	
Sugar	
Sugar, Brown	
Sumac	
Rosemary	
Tahini	
Teriyaki Sauce	
Vanilla Extract	
Vinegar	
Vinegar, Red Wine	
Vinegar, Rice	

SNACKS

ITEM	
Almonds	
Almond Slivers	
Apple Sauce	
Cashews	
Crackers	
Craisins	
Energy Bars	

FOOD INVENTORY

Graham Crackers	
Granola Bars	
Marshmallows	
Olives	
Peanuts	
Peanut Butter	
Peanut Butter Cups	
Pecans	
Pickles	
Pistachio	
Pop Corn	
Potato Chips	
Raisins	
Rice Cake	
Walnuts	

SOUP

ITEM	
Beef and Barley	
Borscht	
Chicken	
Chicken Noodle	
Chili	
Cream of Mushroom	
Lentil	
Matzah Ball	
Miso soup	
Miso Mix	
Mix: Beef	
Mix: Chicken	
Mix: Mushroom	
Mix: Onion	
Mix: Vegetable	
Noodle	
Onion	
Soup Nuts	
Split Pea	
Tomato Soup	
Vegetable	
Vegetable Bean	

PERSONAL INVENTORY

Date Checked ____________ By Whom ____________________

CLEANING

ITEM	
Baby Wipes	
Bleach	
Disinfectant Spray	
Dryer Sheets	
Laundry Detergent	
Rags	
Sanitizer	
Soap	
Toilet Cleaner	

ELECTRIC

ITEM	
9 Volt	
AA	
AAA	
C	
D	
Extension Cord	
Ham Radio	
Walkie Talkie	

FIRST AID

ITEM	
Alcohol	
Allergy Meds	
Aloe Vera Gel	
Ammonia Inhaler	
Antacid	
Aspirin	
Baby Powder	
Band-Aid	
Benadryl Cream	
Benadryl Pills	
Burn Kit	
Calamine Lotion	
Charcoal	
Cotton Balls	
Compound W	
Condoms	
Cough Drops	
Cough Syrup	
Epsom Salt	
Eye Drops	
Fish Antibiotic	
Gauze	
Gloves	
Hemorrhoid Suppositories	
Hydrogen Peroxide	
Ibuprofen	
Ice Packs	
Iodine	
Laxative	
Nasal Spray	
Neosporin	

Poison Ivy	
Saline Solution	
Suture Kit	
Q-Tips	
Tweezers	
Tylenol	
Vaseline	
Which Hazel	

KITCHEN

ITEM	
Aluminum Foil	
Aluminum Foil Sheets	
Bowls, Big	
Bowls, Small	
Bowls, Soup	
Forks	
Knives	
Napkins	
Plastic Wrap	
Paper Towels	
Plates, Big	
Plates, Small	
Soap	
Soup Spoons	
Spoons	
Water Purification Tablets	
Water Straw	
Ziploc Bags, Snack	
Ziploc Bags, Sandwich	
Ziploc Bags, Quart	
Ziploc Bags, Gallon	
Ziploc Bags, 2 Gallon	

LIGHTING

ITEM	
Candles	
Flashlights	
Gasoline	
Glow Sticks	
Lanterns	
Lighter	
Lighter Fluid	
Matches	
Propane	

PERSONAL

ITEM	
Adult Diapers	
Baby Diapers, Cloth	
Baby Diapers, Disposable	
Blindfold	
Earplugs	
Floss	
Hand Warmers	
Insect Repellent	
Lice Shampoo	
Mask	
Medicine	
Mouth Wash	
Mineral Oil	
Nail Polish Remover	
Sewing Kit	
Shampoo	
Sun Block	
Tissues, Box	
Tissues, Cube	
Tissues, Pocket	

Toilet Paper	
Tampons	
Toothbrush	
Toothpaste	

PETS

(Adjust this list to reflect any pets in your home – birds, fish, etc.)

ITEM	
Cat Food	
Cat Toys	
Dog Food	
Dog Toys	
Dog Treats	
Kitty Litter	
Medicine	

PROTECTION

ITEM	
Ammunition	
Blanket	
Flare Gun	
Gun	
Knives	
Mace	
Para Cord	
Rope	
Tactical Pen	

SUPPLIES

ITEM	
Duct Tape	
Sleeping Bag	
Tarp	
Tent	
Trash Bags	

TOOLS

ITEM	
Ax	
Electrical Tape	
File	
Hammer	
Measuring Tape	
Multi-Tool	
Plyers	
Screw Drivers	
Shovel	
Solder	
Soldering Iron	
Teflon Tape	
Voltmeter	
Wire Nuts	
Wrenches	

CONCLUSION

Often life can throw challenges our way and we absolutely must keep our heads. A catastrophe will strain even the most stalwart individual among us. When you have knowledge and training, you will have the fortitude to deal with the situation with calm and equanimity. That is the main reason I took the time and effort to write this book and it may be the very reason you bought and read this work. I am sure it was not for my good looks.

For decades some have preached about a doomsday scenario and others were naysayers saying that nothing was going to happen. In the age of Covid-19, we see that things can change quickly.

With the help of what you have learned herein, you should now be prepared for almost any catastrophe that may come. If something does happen, you will have the knowledge and skills to have peace of mind to prevent yourself from panicking.

As we discussed in several chapters, there are many scenarios for which one could prepare. You should prep for as many scenarios as may apply to you, or for which you are concerned. Stay prepped, and always have a plan; then you can sleep easy knowing no matter, whatever happens, you, and your household would be all right. It is never too late to start, so begin learning the skills required and stocking up on the supplies and food you will need.

Prepping is a way of life and it takes a certain mindset to be able to live and prepare like this. Money that others would use to pay for luxuries, you will be spending on your supplies. Everywhere you turn you will start to notice opportunities for additions to your stash or your knowledge.

There is an old expression that I will paraphrase. “Who is a wise person? The one who sees the future.” We are not prophets nor the children of prophets. However, we have lived through Covid-19 and other situations that lead us to want to prepare for a possible future catastrophe. We cannot see exactly what the future will bring us, however, due to recent events, we can see what may happen and so do what we can to protect our families.

Everyone who is reading this has probably gone without utilities at one time in their lives. It may be due to a storm that the electricity went out; maybe you went camping in a State Forest and tried your hand at primitive style camping, or some other scenario you went without.

My family has been prepping since before Y2K: this was not just a decision we made when the times got bad. We knew days like this were coming upon us and we prepared. A horrible time to begin prepping is when everything is more difficult to come by: it might even be impossible. When the electricity goes out is not the time to purchase a generator. When a storm is on the horizon is not when you should run out, like everyone else, to buy toilet paper and bread.

If this book helps even one person to be prepared for a future catastrophic event, then all my efforts were worthwhile. Start your planning, prepping, and education, and be mindful of events around you.

If this book is well received, I may write a third book on the topics about prepping and surviving in a doomsday scenario.

As I type these words there is another thunderstorm approaching. I am sure nothing untoward will happen, but I will still check my lists and make sure my family is safe.

In conclusion, I hope that you have found this book to be informative and enjoyable. I would like to wish all my readers and their families health, happiness, and safety in all your endeavors. Good luck to you all!

Doomsday
Prepper Lessons
A Prepper's Guide to
Surviving Catastrophe
Ben Jakob

www.ingramcontent.com/pod-product-compliance
Lightning Source LLC
Chambersburg PA
CBHW070533010526
44118CB00012B/1124
* 9 7 8 0 9 9 0 5 8 9 1 7 4 *